S0-BBH-112

WORDLY WISE 3000®

Book 4

Teacher's Resource Book

EDUCATORS PUBLISHING SERVICE
Cambridge and Toronto

Original cover design: Hugh Price
Interior design: Sarah Cole
Acquisitions/Development: Kate Moltz, Lynn Robbins
Editors: Wendy Drexler, Elissa Gershowitz, Stacey Nichols Kim, Theresa Trinder, Laura Woollett
Editorial Assistant: Becky Ticotsky
Senior Editorial Manager: Sheila Neylon

© 2007 by Educators Publishing Service, a division of School Specialty Publishing, a member of the School Specialty Family. All rights reserved. Except as authorized below, no part of this book may be reproduced or utilized in any form or by any electronic or mechanical means, including photocopying, without permission in writing from the publisher.

The purchase of this book entitles the buyer to reproduce designated pages for instructional use. Reproduction for an entire school system or for commercial use is prohibited without written permission.

Printed in USA

ISBN 978-0-8388-2835-9

6 7 8 9 DBH 12 11 10 09

Contents

Program Preface and Components

Words are the tools we use to think, to express ideas and feelings, and to learn about the world. Because words are the very foundation of learning, improving students' vocabulary knowledge has become an educational priority. Student word knowledge is strongly linked with academic accomplishment, because a rich vocabulary is essential to successful reading comprehension. Furthermore, the verbal sections of the high-stakes standardized tests used in most states are basically tests of vocabulary and reading comprehension.

Wordly Wise 3000, Second Edition, has been designed to help students in kindergarten through grade 12 meet state standards for vocabulary and reading comprehension. By using the lessons in the Student Book as well as the tools, strategies, and techniques provided in the Teacher's Resource Book, you can make vocabulary development an effective part of your students' instruction.

Program Components

Student Books (K–12)

Picture Cards (K–1)

Concept Cards (K–1)

Answer Keys (2–12)

Teacher's Resource Books (K–1)

Teacher's Resource Books (2–12)

Teacher's Guide

Student Book Answer Key

Lesson Review Exercises

Lesson Review Answer Key

Tests

Tests Answer Key

Word List

Test Generator (2–12)

The purpose of this Teacher's Resource Book is to provide you with the knowledge and tools you need to increase and improve your students' vocabulary. It begins with the Teacher's Guide, which presents research-based information and proven techniques for vocabulary development as well as specific information and guidelines for using the lessons in Book 4. Following the Guide is an Answer Key to the exercises in the Student Book.

This Teacher's Resource Book also provides review and assessment tools. An additional exercise to use with the Passage is new to the Second Edition and gives you more flexibility in your teaching. You can use it for review or in place of the more challenging final exercise in the lesson. There are also reproducible Tests for each lesson, and Answer Keys for all.

Teacher's Guide

Part 1

What Is Good Vocabulary Development?

Why Vocabulary? Why Teach It?

The *Wordly Wise 3000* series focuses on improving students' vocabulary by furthering their understanding of new words and concepts. Studies have shown that reading comprehension and vocabulary knowledge are strongly correlated,[1] and researchers have found that word knowledge in primary school can predict how well students will be able to comprehend texts they read in high school.[2] Limited vocabularies prevent students from comprehending a text.

Poor readers often read less, because reading is difficult and frustrating for them. This means they don't read enough to improve their vocabularies, which could help them comprehend more. This perpetuating cycle can mean that as students continue through middle school and high school, the gap between good and poor readers grows wider.

Direct instruction in vocabulary can help break this cycle. Good readers often acquire much of their vocabulary through wide independent reading, also known as incidental learning. However, explicit instruction can help students learn enough words to become better readers (and thus acquire even more words). Direct vocabulary instruction is useful for students at all ability levels, but it is particularly useful for beginning students who have a limited reading vocabulary and little exposure to incidental vocabulary learning outside of school.

The average student learns about 3,000 words a year, or six to eight words per day—a remarkable achievement! If students are taught new words at a rate of eight to ten words per week for 37 to 50 weeks, about 300 to 500 words per year can be taught through direct instruction.[3] This leaves a large portion of words to be learned through independent reading, which is essential to acquiring word knowledge.

Although the percentage of words learned through direct instruction may seem small, it is significant. Steven A. Stahl has pointed out that for students at the lower end of the vocabulary range, who learn perhaps 1,000 words a year, a gain of 300 words equals a 30 percent increase, and that for average students a gain of even 10 percent is educationally significant—especially if it is repeated year after year.[4] Experts agree that a combination of direct instruction of word meanings, discussions about words and word parts, and encouragement of wide reading is the best way to help students develop vocabulary.

In this new edition of *Wordly Wise 3000* (K–12), we recommend direct instruction at the primary levels (K–1), more student-centered guidance and coaching at the middle levels (2–6), and more independence at the upper levels (7–12) of the program. Of course, more direct instruction and scaffolding may be warranted at the middle and upper levels with struggling readers and English language learners.

What Should Direct Instruction Include?

So, how do we teach students to acquire words? According to various authorities, effective vocabulary instruction should include definitional and contextual information about a word; multiple exposures to a word in different contexts; and encouragement of students' active participation in their word learning.[5]

Definition and Context

Traditionally, vocabulary instruction has focused on having students look up word meanings and memorize them. This teaching approach, however, provides only superficial and short-term learning of words. Students who simply memorize word meanings frequently have trouble applying the information in definitions and often make mistakes about the meanings.[6]

To know a word, students need to see it in context and learn how its meaning relates to the words around it. An approach that includes definitions as well as context can generate a full and flexible knowledge of word meanings. When students are given several sentences that use a word in different ways, they begin to see how a word's meaning can change and shift depending on its context. For example, consider the changes in the word *got*, as it appears in the following sentences:

> Emilio got a cold.
>
> Emilio got rich.
>
> Emilio got a note from Dashiell.
>
> Dashiell got in trouble.

Although in most of these examples, *got* conveys the idea of receiving, the meaning is slightly different in each one. Based on the concept that students need to see words in different contexts in order to learn them, each lesson in *Wordly Wise 3000* (2–12) provides definitions of the vocabulary words and multiple examples of their use in context.

Repeat, Repeat, and Repeat

Students benefit from seeing the same word several times. Word meanings are accumulated gradually. A word that is encountered once has about a 10 percent chance of being learned from context.[7] When students see a word repeatedly, they gather more and more information about it until they acquire an idea of what it means. Dale and O'Rourke have summarized the four stages of word knowledge as follows:

1. I never saw it before.
2. I've heard of it, but I don't know what it means.
3. I recognize it in context—it has something to do with . . .
4. I know it.[8]

The more exposure students have to a word, the more likely it is that they will be able to define, comprehend, and remember it. Good vocabulary instruction builds repetition into the learning process, so that students can learn more words more quickly. Each lesson in *Wordly Wise 3000* (Books K–12) asks students to use and apply several examples of the lesson's words in different contexts as they complete the exercises.

You Can Do It! Emphasizing Active Processing by Students

Students remember words better when they connect new meanings to knowledge they already have. This type of active processing occurs when students work with words in some of the following ways:

- produce antonyms and synonyms
- rewrite definitions
- identify examples and non-examples of the word
- use more than one new word in a sentence
- create sentences that contain the new word[9]

Each of the above activities reinforces definitional or contextual information about the word and gives students a chance to own the word for themselves. Group discussion of word meanings also helps students learn new vocabulary by having to actively participate in their own learning. More will be said about the importance of discussion in vocabulary instruction in Part 2 of this Guide (see page 13).

How *Wordly Wise 3000* Book 4 Can Help in Vocabulary Development

Each Student Book in the series contains 15 (Books 2–3) to 20 (Books 4–12) lessons. Each lesson teaches 10 (Books 2–3) to 15 (Books 4–12) words and may also teach some variants of a word (such as *magnanimous/magnanimity*). Here is a sample copy of a Book 4 lesson with comments explaining its features.

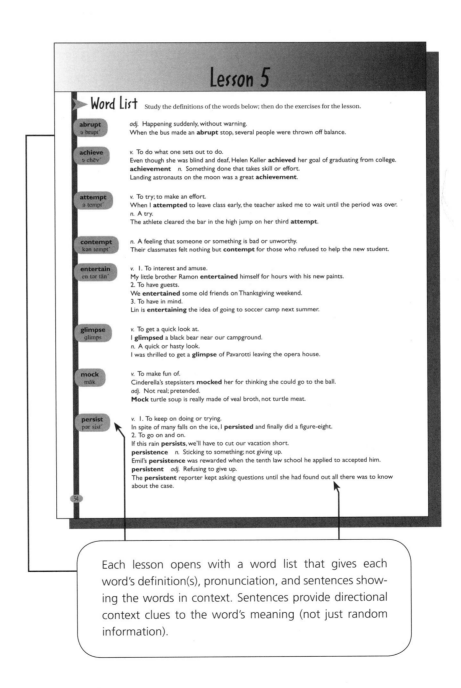

Lesson 5

Word List
Study the definitions of the words below; then do the exercises for the lesson.

abrupt
ə brupt´
adj. Happening suddenly, without warning.
When the bus made an **abrupt** stop, several people were thrown off balance.

achieve
ə chēv´
v. To do what one sets out to do.
Even though she was blind and deaf, Helen Keller **achieved** her goal of graduating from college.
achievement *n.* Something done that takes skill or effort.
Landing astronauts on the moon was a great **achievement**.

attempt
ə tempt´
v. To try; to make an effort.
When I **attempted** to leave class early, the teacher asked me to wait until the period was over.
n. A try.
The athlete cleared the bar in the high jump on her third **attempt**.

contempt
kən tempt´
n. A feeling that someone or something is bad or unworthy.
Their classmates felt nothing but **contempt** for those who refused to help the new student.

entertain
en tər tān´
v. 1. To interest and amuse.
My little brother Ramon **entertained** himself for hours with his new paints.
2. To have guests.
We **entertained** some old friends on Thanksgiving weekend.
3. To have in mind.
Lin is **entertaining** the idea of going to soccer camp next summer.

glimpse
glimps
v. To get a quick look at.
I **glimpsed** a black bear near our campground.
n. A quick or hasty look.
I was thrilled to get a **glimpse** of Pavarotti leaving the opera house.

mock
mäk
v. To make fun of.
Cinderella's stepsisters **mocked** her for thinking she could go to the ball.
adj. Not real; pretended.
Mock turtle soup is really made of veal broth, not turtle meat.

persist
pər sist´
v. 1. To keep on doing or trying.
In spite of many falls on the ice, I **persisted** and finally did a figure-eight.
2. To go on and on.
If this rain **persists**, we'll have to cut our vacation short.
persistence *n.* Sticking to something; not giving up.
Emil's **persistence** was rewarded when the tenth law school he applied to accepted him.
persistent *adj.* Refusing to give up.
The **persistent** reporter kept asking questions until she had found out all there was to know about the case.

34

Each lesson opens with a word list that gives each word's definition(s), pronunciation, and sentences showing the words in context. Sentences provide directional context clues to the word's meaning (not just random information).

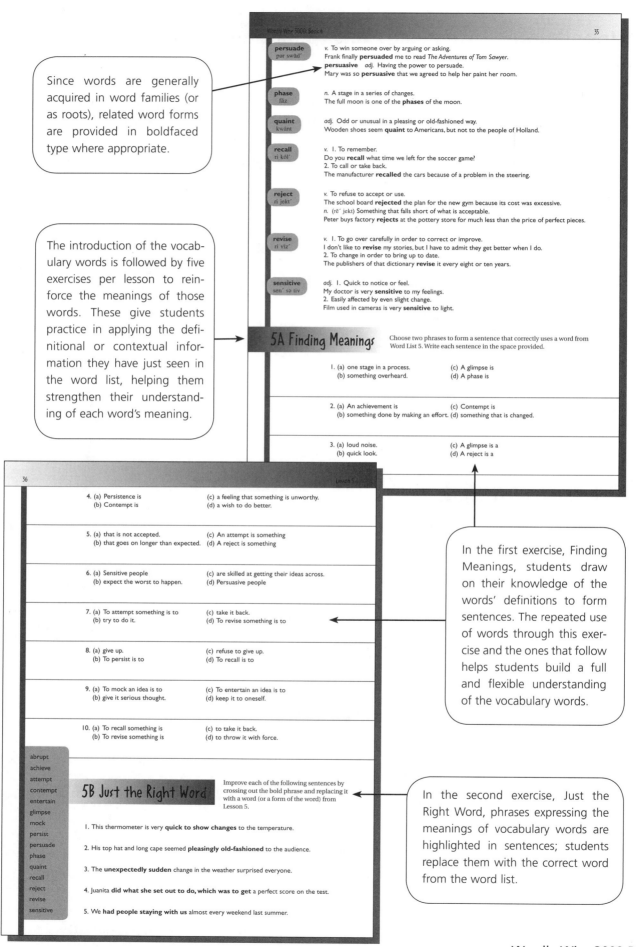

Since words are generally acquired in word families (or as roots), related word forms are provided in boldfaced type where appropriate.

The introduction of the vocabulary words is followed by five exercises per lesson to reinforce the meanings of those words. These give students practice in applying the definitional or contextual information they have just seen in the word list, helping them strengthen their understanding of each word's meaning.

In the first exercise, Finding Meanings, students draw on their knowledge of the words' definitions to form sentences. The repeated use of words through this exercise and the ones that follow helps students build a full and flexible understanding of the vocabulary words.

In the second exercise, Just the Right Word, phrases expressing the meanings of vocabulary words are highlighted in sentences; students replace them with the correct word from the word list.

persuade
pər swād´

v. To win someone over by arguing or asking.
Frank finally **persuaded** me to read *The Adventures of Tom Sawyer*.
persuasive *adj.* Having the power to persuade.
Mary was so **persuasive** that we agreed to help her paint her room.

phase
fāz

n. A stage in a series of changes.
The full moon is one of the **phases** of the moon.

quaint
kwānt

adj. Odd or unusual in a pleasing or old-fashioned way.
Wooden shoes seem **quaint** to Americans, but not to the people of Holland.

recall
ri kôl´

v. 1. To remember.
Do you **recall** what time we left for the soccer game?
2. To call or take back.
The manufacturer **recalled** the cars because of a problem in the steering.

reject
ri jekt´

v. To refuse to accept or use.
The school board **rejected** the plan for the new gym because its cost was excessive.
n. (rē´ jekt) Something that falls short of what is acceptable.
Peter buys factory **rejects** at the pottery store for much less than the price of perfect pieces.

revise
ri vīz´

v. 1. To go over carefully in order to correct or improve.
I don't like to **revise** my stories, but I have to admit they get better when I do.
2. To change in order to bring up to date.
The publishers of that dictionary **revise** it every eight or ten years.

sensitive
sen´ sə tiv

adj. 1. Quick to notice or feel.
My doctor is very **sensitive** to my feelings.
2. Easily affected by even slight change.
Film used in cameras is very **sensitive** to light.

5A Finding Meanings

Choose two phrases to form a sentence that correctly uses a word from Word List 5. Write each sentence in the space provided.

1. (a) one stage in a process.   (c) A glimpse is
   (b) something overheard.   (d) A phase is

2. (a) An achievement is   (c) Contempt is
   (b) something done by making an effort. (d) something that is changed.

3. (a) loud noise.   (c) A glimpse is a
   (b) quick look.   (d) A reject is a

4. (a) Persistence is   (c) a feeling that something is unworthy.
   (b) Contempt is   (d) a wish to do better.

5. (a) that is not accepted.   (c) An attempt is something
   (b) that goes on longer than expected. (d) A reject is something

6. (a) Sensitive people   (c) are skilled at getting their ideas across.
   (b) expect the worst to happen. (d) Persuasive people

7. (a) To attempt something is to (c) take it back.
   (b) try to do it.   (d) To revise something is to

8. (a) give up.   (c) refuse to give up.
   (b) To persist is to   (d) To recall is to

9. (a) To mock an idea is to   (c) To entertain an idea is to
   (b) give it serious thought.   (d) keep it to oneself.

10. (a) To recall something is   (c) to take it back.
    (b) To revise something is   (d) to throw it with force.

abrupt
achieve
attempt
contempt
entertain
glimpse
mock
persist
persuade
phase
quaint
recall
reject
revise
sensitive

5B Just the Right Word

Improve each of the following sentences by crossing out the bold phrase and replacing it with a word (or a form of the word) from Lesson 5.

1. This thermometer is very **quick to show changes** to the temperature.

2. His top hat and long cape seemed **pleasingly old-fashioned** to the audience.

3. The **unexpectedly sudden** change in the weather surprised everyone.

4. Juanita **did what she set out to do, which was to get** a perfect score on the test.

5. We **had people staying with us** almost every weekend last summer.

Wordly Wise 3000 Book 4

6. If the fog **goes on for a long time**, the plane will be unable to leave on time.

7. The coach **made fun of** the shortstop's unusual way of running.

8. I **caught a quick look at** him through the window of the bus.

9. She needs to **make changes in** her speech before she gives it.

10. Each **stage in the series of changes** must be carefully planned or the project will fail.

5C Applying Meanings

Circle the letter of each correct answer to the questions below. A question may have more than one correct answer.

1. Which of the following can be **sensitive**?
   (a) a person's clothing   (c) a person's feelings
   (b) a person's hearing   (d) a person's skin

2. Which of the following might a person think **quaint**?
   (a) a full moon   (c) a hundred-year-old toy
   (b) an old Valentine card   (d) pictures in a 1910 book of fairy tales

3. Which of the following might a person **glimpse**?
   (a) someone leaving a crowded room   (c) a loud noise
   (b) a letter someone is trying to hide   (d) a strange smell

4. Which of the following can a person **achieve**?
   (a) a goal one sets for oneself   (c) curly hair
   (b) a calm frame of mind   (d) high marks on a test

5. Which of the following would you probably **reject**?
   (a) a chance to attend college   (c) bad advice
   (b) an offer of a ride from a stranger   (d) an unworkable plan

6. Which of the following might be **persistent**?
   (a) a flash of lightning   (c) a back pain
   (b) cold and rainy weather   (d) a bad smell

> In Applying Meanings, the third exercise, students answer questions that use the vocabulary words in a specific context. To select the correct answer, students need to use their full knowledge of each word's meaning.

7. Which of the following can be **revised**?
   (a) a written contract   (c) a set of calculations
   (b) a person's height   (d) a weather forecast

8. Which of the following might be **entertaining**?
   (a) a magician's tricks   (c) a bus timetable
   (b) a football game   (d) an aching tooth

5D Word Study

Some things have just one part, and some things have more than one part. A brick has just one part. So does a baseball bat. A box has a bottom, four sides, and a top. Your body is made up of a head, a trunk, and four limbs.

Some words, too, have just one part, and some words have more than one part. There are names for these different parts. The main part of a word is called its *root*. You will remember roots from Lesson 3. Our word *patriotic* is formed from the Latin root *pater*, meaning "father."

A *prefix* is the part of a word that comes before the root. The prefix *un-* turns a word into its opposite. It turns *interesting* into *uninteresting*. *In-* is another prefix that does the same thing. It turns *sane* into *insane*. Note that *in-* changes to *im-* before the *m* sound. This makes it easier to say.

Change each of the words below into its opposite by adding one of the following prefixes: *un-*, *in-*, or *im-*. Check each of your answers in a dictionary to be sure you have formed an actual word.

1. patriotic   _____

2. remarkable   _____

3. mature   _____

4. affected   _____

5. sufficient   _____

6. complete   _____

7. developed   _____

8. persuasive   _____

9. modest   _____

10. sensitive   _____

11. active   _____

12. prepared   _____

Word box: abrupt, achieve, attempt, contempt, entertain, glimpse, mock, persist, persuade, phase, quaint, recall, reject, revise, sensitive

> The fourth exercise provides more sophisticated word study. In the Word Study activity, students may identify synonyms and antonyms, explore how prefixes and suffixes change word meanings, learn about Latin word roots, or distinguish between homophones.

> The vocabulary words appear in a box on every two-page spread in the lesson so that students do not have to flip back to the Word List to see their word choices.

In the final section, Passage, students read an original passage that incorporates all of the vocabulary words from the lesson. The vocabulary words are integral to the understanding of the text and thus contribute to students' comprehension rather than distracting them from the content by focusing on vocabulary. The ultimate goal of the *Wordly Wise 3000* series is to have students develop vocabulary so that they can read with greater fluency.

5E Passage

Read the passage below; then complete the exercise that follows.

A Life That Changed

Hans Christian Andersen's famous story "The Ugly Duckling" tells of a little duckling that looks different from others and is **mocked** by them for being odd. The little creature turns out not to be a duck at all but a beautiful swan. From a quick **glimpse** into the life of the author, we learn that a dramatic change took place in Andersen's own childhood, and that he also took a long time to fit in and to find a special place for himself.

Hans Christian Andersen was born in Denmark in 1805. His father was a shoemaker who struggled to make a living. Hans always felt loved by his parents, and had a happy childhood. He had no brothers or sisters, and he was a **sensitive** child who lived in a private world of his own. His greatest joy was a toy theater his father made for him. The little boy **entertained** his parents by putting on plays, dressing the people of his little toy theater in **quaint** clothes that he made himself.

When Hans was eleven his father died, and the young boy's life changed **abruptly**. He had to go to work, but he failed at every job he **attempted**. His fellow workers could not understand the strange boy who spent all his time daydreaming, and they treated him with **contempt**, making his life miserable. When he was fourteen, Hans **persuaded** his mother to let him go to the big city of Copenhagen, where he tried to get work as an actor, but was unsuccessful. He also tried dancing and singing, but he was not very good at these either. He tried writing plays, but they were **rejected** by theater owners. In this **phase** of his life, he didn't seem to fit in anywhere.

But Hans Christian Andersen **persisted** in his efforts to be a writer. Over the next fifteen years he wrote poems, travel articles, and novels, as well as plays. He worked very hard, taking care to **revise** each sentence carefully until he got the words just right. No one paid much attention to his work, however, until he began writing fairy tales. He did not have to search for ideas for these; all he had to do was **recall** the stories his father had told him when he was a little boy. He wrote more than a hundred and fifty wonderful fairy tales, at last **achieving** fame and becoming one of the best-loved writers in the world. You will read one of his stories in the next lesson.

Answer each of the following questions in the form of a sentence. If a question does not contain a vocabulary word from this lesson's word list, use one in your answer. Use each word only once. Questions and answers will then contain all fifteen words (or forms of the words).

1. How do you think a **sensitive** person like Andersen might have responded to cruel remarks?

2. What was one of Andersen's favorite childhood activities?

3. Why did the people in Hans's toy theater look so charmingly old-fashioned?

4. What caused an **abrupt** change in Andersen's life when he was a child?

5. What might Andersen have said to **persuade** his mother to let him go to Copenhagen?

6. Why must Andersen's mother have been pessimistic about his chances of success?

7. How do you know that Andersen was not popular with his fellow workers?

8. Was Andersen's playwriting successful?

9. What jobs did Hans try during the **phase** of his life when he didn't fit in anywhere?

10. In your opinion, what was Andersen's greatest **achievement**?

11. What helped give Andersen ideas for stories?

12. How can you tell that Andersen was usually not satisfied with his first version of a story?

13. What quality did Andersen have that helped him succeed?

After reading the passage, students answer questions about it. If a vocabulary word is not used in the question, students must use it in their response. In this way, each word is reviewed once again. Although the questions are about the content of the passage, students need to understand the meanings of the vocabulary words in order to be able to answer them.

14. Why do you think the people Andersen worked with mocked him?

15. Why might the story of the Ugly Duckling be of special interest to Andersen's readers?

FUN & FASCINATING FACTS

The Latin *abruptus* means "broken" and forms the root of the adjective **abrupt**. If there is an *abrupt* end to something—a speech, for example—it means it was *broken* off suddenly and unexpectedly.

Other words formed from this root include *interrupt* (When you *interrupt* a conversation, you *break* into it) and *disrupt* (If you *disrupt* a meeting, you *break* it up).

The *Wordly Wise 3000* lessons work sequentially, with each exercise requiring more precise knowledge of the vocabulary words than the previous exercise. This systematic approach to vocabulary instruction enables students to actively participate in the process of their own word learning by thinking about the various meanings of each word and applying what they know.

A boxed feature called Fun & Fascinating Facts appears at the end of each lesson. This feature provides explanations or short stories about word origins and word families. Telling stories about words conveys a sense of fun about language and encourages students to become interested in learning words in general.

Review for Lessons 5–8

Crossword Puzzle Solve the crossword puzzle below by studying the clues and filling in the answer boxes. Clues followed by a number are definitions of vocabulary words in Lessons 5 through 8. The number gives the lesson from which the answer to the clue is taken.

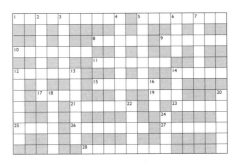

Clues Across

1. To give out (7)
5. To win over by arguing or asking (5)
8. To change in some way (7)
9. An animal that is being hunted (8)
10. The topmost part; the outer layer (8)
11. A part or share of the whole (8)
12. Twice as much
14. Each separate item on a list (8)
15. Skilled at tricking others (6)
17. Dull and without color (6)
19. Adam and _____
21. To make pure (6)
23. To take by force of the law (7)
25. Eight, _____ , ten
26. A large room (8)
27. Having nothing left out (6)
28. Place where something is (8)

Clues Down

2. To be around on all sides (7)
3. To remember (5)
4. To interest and amuse (5)
5. To go on longer than expected (5)
6. Opposite of *open*
7. Happening suddenly without warning (5)
12. To go to a lower level (8)
13. To hold closely (7)
14. Used to see with
16. Opposite of *no*
18. To say you won't accept (5)
20. Very strict or harsh
22. To throw out (7)
24. Showing a strong interest; eager (7)

Every fourth lesson is followed by a crossword puzzle or hidden message puzzle that incorporates the words from the previous four lessons, giving students a playful way to revisit the words they now know as their own.

How, When, and Where to Use *Wordly Wise 3000*

Wordly Wise 3000 (Books 2–12) is designed for maximum flexibility. The lessons included in the books can be used in different settings (in class, at home, in one-on-one tutoring sessions), at different frequencies (once a week, three times a week, every day), and in varied sequences (lessons can be followed in numerical order or used individually). The teachers who use these books with their students have told us they use them in several different ways:

- as in-class activities
- as homework
- as independent study
- as preparation for standardized tests or spelling bees

We recognize that many teachers have students with different reading levels in their classrooms. The *Wordly Wise 3000* series can help a teacher accommodate these differences. By choosing the appropriate level of the *Wordly Wise 3000* books for particular students, teachers can ensure that their advanced students stay challenged and their struggling students have material that suits their learning level.

Our research shows that about half of the teachers working with *Wordly Wise 3000* teach vocabulary two or three times per week. About a third teach vocabulary almost every day, and ten percent teach vocabulary once a week. (Percentages do not add up to 100 because some teachers did not answer this question in our survey or chose "other.") The *Wordly Wise 3000* series can accommodate these individual schedules. Here are some typical plans.

Once-a-Week Teaching Plan

If you are able to devote only one class per week to vocabulary, it is best to use that time to help students become familiar enough with the new words that they can complete the exercises outside of class on their own. Such a teaching plan might look like this:

Vocabulary Day
As a class, go over the word list thoroughly. Have students read the definitions and sample sentences aloud. Ask students to use the new words in sentences of their own. Use queries, illustrations, pantomimes, and graphic organizers (described in Part 2 of this Guide, page 13) to encourage discussion of what a word means and how it differs from related words. Make a Word Wizard chart (see Part 2) that contains all the week's vocabulary words and display it in the classroom. Ask students to be on the lookout for the words outside the classroom. When they encounter one of them, they can add their names to the chart with their examples of how each word was used. Assign all or a selection of the exercises in the lesson as homework for the following week.

Three-Days-a-Week Teaching Plan

Teachers who can devote three days a week to vocabulary instruction should be able to complete one lesson each week, with students doing most of the exercises in the student book and some of the activities and enrichments suggested in the Teacher's Guide. Such a teaching plan might look like this:

Day 1

Introduce the word list to the class and facilitate discussion about each item. Complete the Finding Meanings exercise as a group. Assign the Just the Right Word and Applying Meanings exercises as homework to be ready by the next vocabulary class day.

Day 2

Refresh the students' memories about the words in the lesson by asking volunteers to briefly define each one. Review the homework as a group, having students explain why one answer is correct and the others wrong. Have a student or students read the Passage aloud. Assign the Word Study and Passage questions as homework to be ready by the next *Wordly Wise 3000* class day.

Day 3

Review the homework as a group, again having the class discuss what makes the correct answer correct. Reinforce the students' new knowledge by having them pick five words from the list to use in a short story or essay on any topic.

Five-Days-a-Week Teaching Plan

Teachers who teach vocabulary every day should be able to complete one lesson each week, with students doing all the exercises in the student book and many of the activities and enrichments suggested in the Teacher's Guide. Such a teaching plan might look like this:

Day 1

Introduce the word list to the class and facilitate discussion about each item. Use queries, illustrations, pantomimes, and graphic organizers (described in Part 2 of this Guide, pp. 13–24) to encourage discussion of what a word means and what it doesn't mean. Assign the Finding Meanings exercise as homework to be ready by the next class day.

Day 2

Review the homework as a group, having students explain why one answer is correct and the others wrong. Have the students complete the Just the Right Word exercise in small groups, then discuss the answers as a class.

Day 3

Complete the Applying Meanings and Word Study exercises by calling on students to answer questions one at a time. Query the class to gauge their understanding, and solicit explanations from other class members to clarify meanings.

Day 4

Have the students read the Passage and answer the questions that follow on their own. Discuss the answers as a class.

Day 5

Have the students demonstrate their mastery of the new words by paraphrasing—rewriting definitions for the words, using the words in their own sentences or stories, or both.

A Final Word: How Instruction Can Help Students Who Start with Smaller Vocabularies

Students come to school with vastly different vocabularies. Some will know thousands more word meanings than other students in your class. This occurs in part because of the differences in the number of new words students are exposed to in their homes and communities. Students who come from homes where spoken and written vocabularies are limited will know fewer words than students who come from homes where exposure to a wide range of vocabulary is common. Arriving in class with a small vocabulary does not predict failure—it only highlights the need for direct vocabulary instruction in the schools. As one researcher put it:

> If we are serious about "increasing standards" and bringing a greater proportion of schoolchildren to high levels of academic accomplishment, we cannot continue to leave vocabulary development to parents, chance, and highly motivated reading.[10]

Studies have shown that the key to increasing vocabulary is exposure to new words, not an innate ability to learn from context.[11] Experts emphasize that vocabulary development is an attainable goal. If given the opportunity to learn new words as well as effective instruction, most students can acquire vocabulary at rates that will improve their comprehension. This enables them to read increasingly challenging texts with fluency and improves their chances for success in school and afterward.

Part 2

General Strategies and Specific Techniques for Teaching Vocabulary

Other Aspects of Good Vocabulary Development

Effective vocabulary development is a multifaceted process requiring a combination of direct instruction, discussion, and active encouragement of independent learning strategies. On their own and in the classroom, students draw on a variety of methods to learn the thousands of words they acquire each year. This part of the Guide will discuss the following general strategies and specific techniques to keep in mind as you teach vocabulary:

- encouraging wide reading
- emphasizing learning from context
- using prefixes, suffixes, and roots
- using graphic organizers such as semantic maps, concept of definition maps, semantic feature analysis, and Venn diagrams
- extending instruction through reading aloud and discussion

These approaches will enhance your vocabulary curriculum and can be used to supplement the direct instruction that *Wordly Wise 3000* provides.

Volumes of Volumes: Encouraging Wide Reading

Getting your students to read more may be the most valuable thing you can do to improve their vocabulary. Although direct instruction plays a crucial part in vocabulary growth, most of the words your students learn will be acquired through incidental learning, as they read on their own. The average student learns about 3,000 words a year. Although direct instruction plays a crucial part in vocabulary growth, evidence shows that wide reading is the main avenue for student word acquisition. Researchers present this scenario to demonstrate the effectiveness of wide reading:[12]

- If, over a school year, a fifth-grader reads for an hour each day, five days a week, in and out of school at a conservative rate of 150 words per minute, the student will encounter 2,250,000 words in the course of reading.

- If 2 to 5 percent of the words the student encounters are unknown words, he or she will encounter from 45,000 to 112,500 new words.

- We know that students learn between 5 and 10 percent of previously unknown words from a single reading. Using the lower number given above for unknown words encountered during the reading program, we see that a student would learn at least 2,250 new words from context each year.

This estimate suggests that incidental learning is critical to vocabulary development. Again, the more students read, the more word meanings they will know and the more likely they will be to read with both pleasure and comprehension.

To be truly beneficial, wide reading should include texts with varied levels of difficulty. Students reading at or below their current levels will not dramatically increase their vocabulary. And as you know, when students read texts that consist primarily of unknown words, they usually become frustrated. To help them get the most out of incidental learning, you should have them read some books for fun and others for a challenge.

Motivating students to read can be a difficult task. Here are a few suggestions for making reading appealing to students at all ability levels:

- Devote some class time to independent silent reading. This time may be particularly helpful for students who have never done extensive reading for pleasure. Reading for a length of time in class will enable students to do this on their own outside of class.

- Make a variety of books available in class and recommend books for students to find in the library and to read outside of class. You might want to provide lists of books students might like to read.

- Promote social interactions related to reading. Setting a time for regular discussions of books students have read will motivate them to read more and help them understand their reading better. (See page 23 in the final section of Part 2 for more about the importance of discussion.)

- Model the importance you place on reading by telling students about books you are reading. When students have silent reading time, read a book of your own to show that reading is a valuable activity that you enjoy, too.

These strategies will have long-term benefits for your students. Wide reading is a key component to vocabulary development, but as with much important learning, its effects are cumulative rather than immediate. The next sections will discuss what you can do to help students get the most out of reading actively and efficiently.

Getting a Clue: Emphasizing Learning from Context

Most of the words acquired through incidental reading are learned through context. Students learn from context by making connections between the new word and the text in which it appears. As noted in Part 1 of this Guide, students learn words through repeated exposures, gaining more comprehension of a word's meanings and functions by seeing it several times in different contexts.

Experts debate the effectiveness of teaching students how to use context clues. While some studies show that teaching students how to identify and use context clues is an effective technique for increasing vocabulary,[13] other research suggests that learning words from context is an innate skill that all readers use. Kuhn and Stahl have found that children of all abilities learn at the same rate from context; that is, advanced readers are no more efficient at learning from context than less advanced readers—the advanced readers simply read more.[14] All experts, however, stress that it is crucial to make students aware of the importance of using context clues as an essential tool in word acquisition.

Here are some techniques for enhancing students' awareness of the importance of context clues:[15]

- Model basic strategies for using context clues, when working with *Wordly Wise 3000* or reading other texts.
- Provide explanations of how, when, and why to use context to figure out word meanings.
- Provide guided practice in using context.
- Remind students to apply the skill when reading.

You can also use activities such as the Word Wizard chart (developed by Beck, et al.) to make students aware of learning words in context.[16] As you discuss unfamiliar words in class, you can add them to the chart. If a student comes across the word again when reading and notes its context, his or her name goes up on the chart. You can provide students with periodic rewards for being Word Wizards (that is, contributing many words to the chart).

Another way to emphasize the importance of learning from context is to have students rate their knowledge of a new word by using a checklist, as shown on page 16:

Knowledge Rating Checklist
How much do I know about these words?

	Can define	Have seen/heard	Don't know
conclude		✓	
elder	✓		
forlorn			✓
hearty		✓	
inhale	✓		
merit	✓		
stingy	✓		
summon		✓	
valient			✓

These checklists can also be used in group activities in class. You may also want to have students keep these checklists together in a notebook along with a running list of words they come across that intrigue or interest them. Encouraging a general awareness of words as fun and interesting in themselves will help students pursue their own vocabulary development.

Using context is an important skill that students will employ frequently. However, in learning when to use context clues, students also need to know when not to use this strategy. Since many texts do not signal the meanings of words explicitly, using context is not always the best way to derive the meanings of new words. The next two sections will discuss how to teach other strategies for increasing word knowledge.

Part Smart: Using Prefixes, Suffixes, and Roots

Experts have noted that the upper elementary grades are a good time to start teaching students how to use word parts to figure out the meanings of words.[17] Information from prefixes, suffixes, and roots can help students learn and remember words; using word parts can be a particularly useful strategy in reading content-area texts. For example, science texts will often include words that use the same word parts repeatedly, such as *bio-* in *bio-sphere, biology, biodegradable, bioluminescence,* and *biochemical.* Knowing that "bio" means life can help students recognize these words in context and add to their comprehension of these words. (This particular root will also help students learn words across content areas. For example, in language arts students will encounter words such as *biography*.)

You can begin to teach word-part strategy by telling students that words can be composed of affixes—prefixes and suffixes—and roots. Learning to break words into affixes and roots will make some long words more manageable for students who may be intimidated by the length of words such as *interdependent*. Modeling how to break words into parts may be necessary. To do this, you can teach students to cover prefixes such as *inter-* in the word *interdependent*, and see if they recognize the rest of the word. Then you can have them cover the suffix *-ent*, leaving *depend*.[18] Further modeling and practice with adding and removing prefixes and suffixes such as *un-* and *-able* will give students facility with breaking words down into parts.

In teaching word parts, you should stress how the parts function to affect word meaning. You may want to point out that prefixes such as *un-*, *super-*, *anti-*, *mis-*, and *sub-* change the meanings of the roots they precede in predictable ways. Since prefixes are consistently defined, you may want to supply definitions of the prefixes given in the table below.

The Most Frequent Affixes in Printed School English

Rank	Prefix	% of All Prefixed Words	Suffix	% of All Suffixed Words
1.	un-	26	-s, -es	31
2.	re-	14	-ed	20
3.	in-, im-, il-, ir- (not)	11	-ing	14
4.	dis-	7	-ly	7
5.	en-, em-	4	-er, -or (agent)	4
6.	non-	4	-ion, -tion, -ation, -ition	4
7.	in-, im- (in)	3	-able, -ible	2
8.	over-	3	-al, -ial	1
9.	mis-	3	-y	1
10.	sub-	3	-ness	1
11.	pre-	3	-ity, -ty	1
12.	inter-	3	-ment	1
13.	fore-	3	-ic	1
14.	de-	2	-ous, -eous, -ious	1
15.	trans-	2	-en	1
16.	super-	1	-er (comparative)	1
17.	semi-	1	-ive, -ative, -tive	1
18.	anti-	1	-ful	1
19.	mid-	1	-less	1
20.	under- (too little)	1	-est	1
	All Others	3	All Others	1

Suffixes have less stable meanings, so merely learning their abstract definitions can be confusing. But learning to recognize common suffixes such as *-tion, -less, -ed,* and *-ing* will help students know a word's function. For example, remembering that *-tion* indicates the word is a noun and that *-ed* usually forms the past tense of verbs can make it easier for readers to figure out words using these suffixes. Providing plenty of examples of suffixed words is probably more useful than memorizing the definitions of suffixes.[19]

Once students have grasped the concepts of prefixes, suffixes, and roots, you can easily teach them specific word parts. Only 20 prefixes make up 97 percent of the prefixed words in printed school English. Sixty-five percent of suffixed words end in *-s, -es, -ed,* or *-ing.*[20] The table on page 17 shows a list of the most commonly used prefixes and suffixes used in printed school English. Teaching your students to use just a few of these affixes can dramatically improve their vocabulary development. One study found that third graders who were taught the first nine prefixes in the chart and how to break down words into roots and suffixes outperformed a control group tested in measures of word meaning.[21]

Many lists containing hundreds of Greek and Latin roots are available, but teaching the meanings of roots may not be as useful to your students as teaching the affixes. Some researchers have pointed out that the current meanings of many words do not resemble their historical roots. Trying to apply the ancient meanings of roots to figure out the meanings of words used today is difficult but often worth doing

However, telling students about the roots of words they are learning can help make those words more memorable by adding a story to what they know. For example, the following account of the origin of *century* from the Fun & Fascinating Facts feature in Lesson 8 reinforces the word's meaning:

> A large number of English words are formed from Greek or Latin numbers. Among them is our word **century**, a period of one hundred years. It comes from the Latin for one hundred, which is *centum.* Other words sharing this root include *cent* (there are one hundred cents in a dollar), *centipede* (this creature was once thought to have one hundred legs, but it actually has about seventy), and *centimeter* (there are one hundred *centimeters* in a meter).

In content areas such as science, it may be useful to have students memorize roots that recur. Using word webs like the one on page 19 can reinforce the relations among words incorporating these roots.

Word Part Web

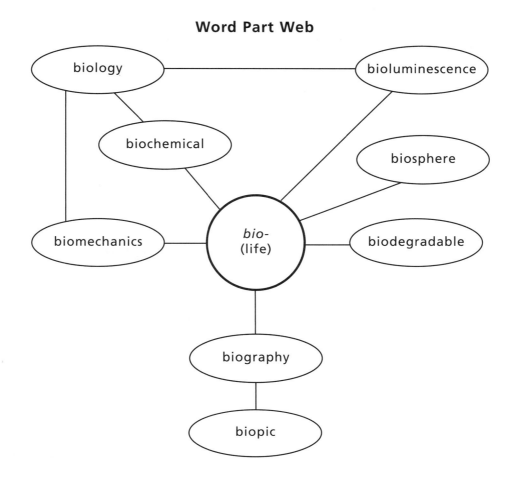

The strategy of using word parts is probably most effective when combined with other ways of acquiring words, such as context clues. Knowing how to break down words into parts will make them easier to tackle; learning prefixes, suffixes, and some roots will give students more tools for vocabulary growth.

I See What You Mean: Using Graphic Organizers

Encouraging wide reading, using context, and employing word parts are excellent long-term strategies for vocabulary development. This section provides some additional activities that can deepen your students' word knowledge and expand your direct instruction of vocabulary.

Concept of Definition Maps

Concept of definition maps such as the one on this page are graphic organizers that show the elements of a typical dictionary definition, including:

- The category to which the word belongs, labeled, "What is this?"
- Characteristics of the word, labeled, "What is it like?"
- Examples and non-examples of the word.[22]

Students fill in the maps by referring to context, using their prior knowledge, and consulting dictionaries. The following map elucidates the meaning of *portion,* which appears in Lesson 8:

Concept of Definition Map

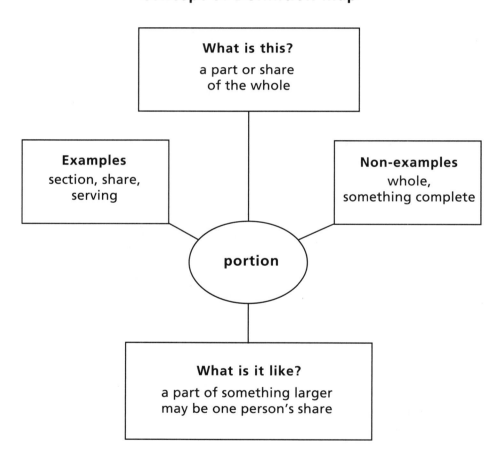

After having the class complete the map, you may want to model how to write a definition using the information in the map. For example, you could say: "A *portion* is a part or share of a whole. It might be a section of something or one person's serving of food." You can also have students write their own definitions and then confirm them by looking the word up in the dictionary. They may revise their definitions after looking them up.

Semantic Maps

Semantic maps can be used to develop students' understanding of a particular concept or group of thematically related words.[23] For example, in teaching an essay about the Great Wall of China, you might target the following vocabulary words: *barrier, threat, external, frontier,* and *breadth.* Then, you may begin instruction by having students brainstorm words that are related to the concept. As they brainstorm, you list their words on the board, making sure to include the words you have targeted for them to learn.

Discussion is key to semantic mapping. During the brainstorming session, have students discuss and define all of the words on the list. Help students refine their understanding of the words by asking them to group related words together to create a semantic map such as this one:

Semantic Map

The target words are highlighted, and sections are left blank so that the class can fill in another category after reading the selection. Semantic mapping is a good technique to use in content-area teaching, in which vocabulary words will be thematically related. The technique works best as a group activity, since discussion will help students with smaller vocabularies learn all the words that are talked about. Advanced learners will benefit from the extra exposure to words they have learned.

Semantic Feature Analysis

Another good technique to use in teaching words that share content is semantic feature analysis, which makes use of a grid, such as the one below.[24] The left-hand column contains the names of members of the category. For a unit on living creatures, you might write words such as: *dog, cat, hamster, buffalo, tiger, sparrow,* and *horse.* The top row of the grid lists features of the category's members such as: *has fur, has feathers, can fly, can be a pet,* and *runs on four legs.* Students should be encouraged to add terms to either the column or the row during discussion.

Semantic Feature Analysis

	has fur	has feathers	can fly	can be a pet	runs on four legs
dog	+	-	-	+	+
cat	+	-	-	+	+
hamster	+	-	-	+	+
buffalo	?	-	-	-	+
tiger	+	-	-	-	+
sparrow	-	+	+	-	-
horse	?	-	-	?	+

After seeing the grid, groups of students or the whole can class discuss whether the items in the column are an example of the features across the top, marking **+** for positive examples, **–** for negative examples, and **?** for words that *might* be examples.

As with semantic maps, discussion is key to clarifying the meanings of words in this activity. It is also an excellent technique to use in content areas such as social studies and science.

Comparing and Contrasting: Venn Diagrams

Venn diagrams are another good graphic organizer to use, especially when teaching students to compare and contrast related concepts such as *trip* and *sojourn, virus* and *bacteria, nation* and *country,* and *poetry* and *prose.* The following diagram helps to clarify the similarities and differences between two related ideas:

Venn Diagram

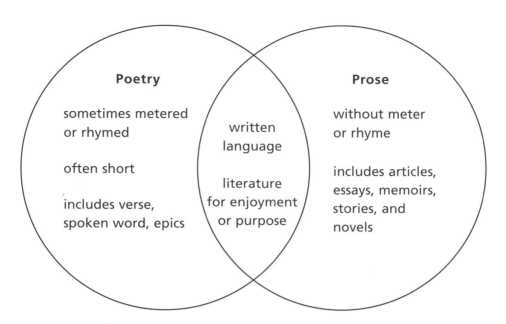

Poetry

sometimes metered
or rhymed

often short

includes verse,
spoken word, epics

written
language

literature
for enjoyment
or purpose

Prose

without meter
or rhyme

includes articles,
essays, memoirs,
stories, and
novels

Using graphic organizers will provide your students with more exposures to words they are acquiring and will help them solidify the knowledge they've gained. The final section will discuss how oral language can be used to enhance your vocabulary instruction even further.

Let's Talk: Extending Instruction through Reading Aloud and Discussion

Reading literature to students exposes them to rich language, sometimes referred to as "book language," that they usually do not hear in everyday speech. Reading nonfiction materials aloud to students exposes them to domain words—those words associated with a particular content area—that they need to be successful in school. The *Wordly Wise 3000* series provides a rich array of both types of words at all levels.

Reading aloud is a common practice in the lower grades; in fact, reading aloud, in conjunction with using picture cues, forms the basis for *Wordly Wise 3000* K–1. Although research states that reading volume, rather than oral language, is the prime contributor to differences in students' vocabularies past the fourth grade,[25] additional research indicates that sixth graders learned about as many words from a single listening as they would from a single reading.[26] Therefore, reading aloud can be a beneficial strategy to use even with older students, especially struggling readers, English language learners, and those who have smaller vocabularies.

Discussion can greatly enhance any vocabulary instruction. Students with small vocabularies benefit from the knowledge contributed by their classmates, and misunderstandings of words can be cleared up publicly. In addition, as students wait to be called on, they often practice responses silently. As a result, discussion reinforces vocabulary development.[27] Discussions can be made more fun by having students act out or pantomime words or engage in debates about word meanings.

Since vocabulary growth is such a long process, drawing on a variety of approaches will help prevent boredom. Some words will require much more detailed instruction than others; certain activities such as semantic maps work best with words that are related in meaning. As you experiment with the strategies and techniques just described, you will be able to determine which ones will best help your students. The last part of this Guide will demonstrate how you can use some of these approaches as you teach *Wordly Wise 3000* lessons.

Part 3

Sample Lesson

This part of the Guide provides instruction and modeling of how to teach a sample lesson in Book 4. These instructions will help you introduce the basic concepts and approaches used in the lessons and will also help you extend the lessons, using the strategies and techniques discussed in Part 2. These approaches presented will work no matter what level you are teaching. If you have not taught a *Wordly Wise 3000* lesson before, the following sample lesson instructions will give you an understanding of the format and purpose of all *Wordly Wise 3000* lessons.

Lesson 1

Word List

Begin by having students look at the word list for this lesson. Tell them that each lesson in *Wordly Wise 3000* Book 4 opens with a list of 15 words that they will discuss and learn, and that the word list will be followed by several exercises.

Tell students that each word list provides definitions of the words as well as examples of how the words are used in sentences. You may want to discuss the word list as a class. Point out that each word's pronunciation is given beneath it and that each definition includes the word's part of speech. Tell them that often a word will take more than one form, as in the first word, *benefit*, which is defined as both a verb and a noun. Also tell them that the words will often have more than one meaning.

---

benefit
be´ nə fit

v. To help or be helpful to; to be useful to.
That preschool program **benefits** young children.
n. 1. Something that is useful or helpful, that does good.
One of the **benefits** of my exercise program is that I sleep better.
2. An event held to raise money for a cause.
The library's **benefit** raised enough money for a new children's room.

Read aloud each definition and sentence for *benefit* and have students ask questions about the meanings. You may want to point out that the example sentences usually contain context clues to the meanings of the words. For example, for the noun form of *benefit,* the phrase "that I sleep better" provides an example of what a *benefit* is. Remind students that context clues can help them understand a word's meaning. Again, since this is the first lesson, you may want to go through all the words in the word list in a similar manner, reading the definitions and sentences aloud and having students discuss the words. In subsequent lessons, you can have students study the words on their own.

To reinforce the meanings of some words such as *hail* or *remark,* you may want to illustrate them on the board or pantomime the actions. Note that sometimes several versions of a word will be given in boldface type, as with *patriot, patriotic,* and *patriotism.*

You can extend the introduction of some words by using a concept of definition map. To use this technique with *utter,* draw a blank map on the board as shown below:

Concept of Definition Map

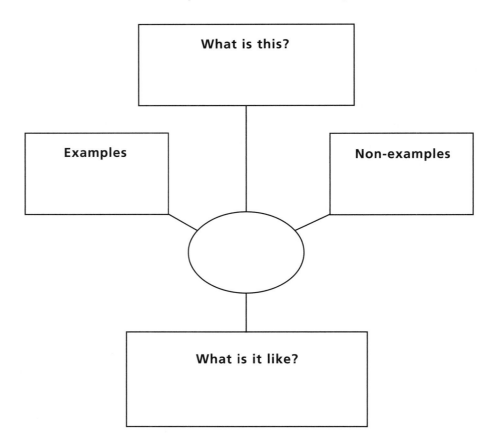

Wordly Wise 3000 Book 4

Have students read the definition of *utter,* and then as a class, have them answer the questions in each box. You may want to instruct students to consult the dictionary to supplement their knowledge of the word. Write their answers in the boxes, as shown below:

Concept of Definition Map

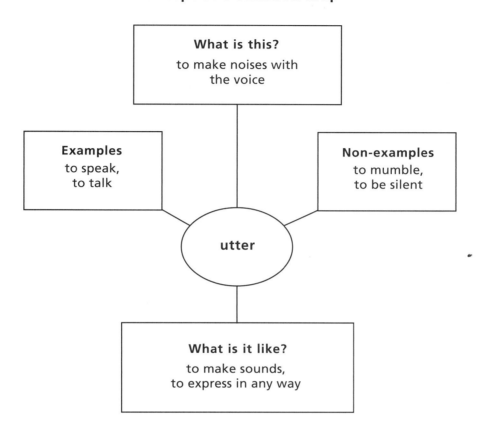

Then, model how to write a complete definition of the word, using the map. For example, you could say: "To utter is to speak or make sounds with the voice. When you utter, you express sounds that other people can hear." This map reinforces word meanings and can be used to provide students with extra practice with a word at any point in a lesson.

1A Finding Meanings

In the first exercise, students draw on their knowledge of the words' definitions to form sentences. Tell students that they should pick two of the four phrases to form a sentence that makes sense. Remind them that they can use the definitions of the words on the previous pages to answer these items.

For item 1, you can model the exercise by telling students to begin by looking at the four options: a, b, c, and d. Ask them, "Which two options can begin a sentence?" Say that since b and c begin with capital letters and can start the sentence, they should try combining these two options with the remaining ones to see if they make sense. You can write the following sentences on the board:

- Hail is a useful aid.
- Hail is frozen rain.
- Dismay is a useful aid.
- Dismay is frozen rain.

Have students discuss the sentences and choose the correct answer ("Hail is frozen rain."). As a class, have students complete the rest of the items in 1A, and answer any questions students have about the exercise.

1B Just the Right Word

In the second exercise, Just the Right Word, students replace definitions of the words as they appear in sentences with the correct vocabulary words. Tell students that the word list is repeated in the box on this page. They should review it to familiarize themselves with the possible choices.

Read the instructions aloud and write the first sentence on the board. Read this sentence aloud and ask students what word from the list replaces or is a synonym for "total absence." Cross out this phrase and write *lack* above it. You may want to repeat these steps with several items and then have students complete the rest of the exercise on their own.

You can extend this activity by having students come up with antonyms for some of the words, after they have completed the exercise. Not all words have antonyms, of course, but thinking about antonyms requires students to consider crucial aspects of a word. In this exercise, you might have students identify the antonyms for *lack, complete,* and *dismayed.* Possible antonyms include: *abundance, unfinished, happy.*

1C Applying Meanings

In Applying Meanings, students choose correct answers to questions involving the vocabulary words. This exercise requires students to use their knowledge of each word's meaning and apply it in new contexts.

Read aloud the instructions and remind students that they can circle more than one answer. Then have a volunteer read the first question and the possible answers. Have the class discuss whether or not and why each answer might be correct. Although a and c are the most probable answers to item 1, some students might be dismayed at finding celery in a tuna sandwich! Discussion will help students clarify the subtle meanings of the vocabulary words and will make this exercise more lively. To get the most out of discussion, it's a good idea to call on many different students, so that the majority of the class will be silently preparing answers. You may wish to extend discussion throughout the exercise or have students complete the exercise on their own.

1D Word Study

The fourth exercise provides students with more sophisticated word study. The Word Study activity alternates among several types of exercises: synonyms and antonyms, prefixes and suffixes, Latin and Greek word roots, and homophones.

Exercise 1D in Book 4 introduces synonyms. Read the instructions aloud. Discuss the examples *big* and *large*. Ask students if they know any other words with similar meanings, such as *huge* and *massive*, and discuss the gradations of meaning of the words. Then discuss the meaning of *synonym*.

Read aloud the first set of words. Ask the class which items are synonymous, or have similar meanings. Use discussion to clarify the meanings of the words and the correct answer: *benefit* and *help*. Remind students to circle those words. Repeat this step with several items and then have students complete the exercise on their own. You can follow a similar pattern with the other Word Study exercises in this book.

1E Passage

In the final section, Passage, students read an original passage that incorporates the vocabulary words. By this point, students have become well acquainted with the meanings of the words, so that the reading in context is in effect "debugged" for them. Most of the passages are nonfiction and cover the content areas of science, math, and social studies.

The vocabulary words are integral to the understanding of the text, and thus contribute to students' understanding of the passage. The ultimate goal of *Wordly Wise 3000* is to have students develop vocabulary so that they can read with greater fluency.

After reading the passage, students answer questions about it. Students must use complete sentences to answer the questions, and more subtle knowledge of how a word adapts to its context is required to answer some of these questions.

Depending on your students' needs, you may want to read the passage aloud, "Sequoya's Gift." Then read the instructions that follow the passage and clarify any questions students have about the exercise. Have the class work together to answer the first three items. Remind students that sometimes, as in question 3, they must use a vocabulary word in the answer, since none is used in the question. Have students complete the remaining exercises on their own or in small groups.

In *Wordly Wise 3000*, Second Edition, an alternative exercise has been provided. It can be found in this Teacher's Resource Book beginning on page 43. While it is titled "Lesson Review Exercise," this cloze exercise can be used as a less challenging follow-up to the Passage, as a lesson extension (see below), or for review or assessment. Read the directions with students, and walk them through the first item, discussing their answers.

1E Extending the Lesson

To extend this final exercise and the lesson as a whole, you may wish to use the Lesson Review Exercise discussed above. You may also encourage students to write short passages using words from the list.

After students have completed all the exercises, point out the Fun & Fascinating Facts feature, which provides explanations or short stories about word origins and word families. Explain that English words are often derived from Latin, Greek, and other roots, which can sometimes help students figure out word meanings. Volunteers may read the feature aloud.

Tell students that every fourth lesson is followed by a crossword or hidden message puzzle that uses the words from the previous four lessons.

You will know best how much modeling and guidance your students will need to complete each lesson. You can also use the preceding instructions to teach students how to do most of the lessons in Book 4.

Testing and Assessment

When your students have completed a lesson in *Wordly Wise 3000* (2–12), assess their understanding by administering the corresponding Lesson Test. These reproducible tests, found in this Teacher's Resource Book beginning on page 69, test every word in all the forms and meanings presented in *Wordly Wise 3000*. In addition, a cumulative Midterm (following Lesson 10) and a Final Test (following Lesson 20) each provide a new passage using a selection of the words from the previous lessons. The new passages help ensure that students can apply the word meanings they have learned in a different context. An Answer Key for the Lesson, Midterm, and Final Tests can be found on page 205.

As an alternative, you may wish to use the *Wordly Wise 3000* Test Generator, available separately. The Test Generator allows you to customize your assessment by choosing only those words you wish to test, as well as providing you the opportunity to test words from a group of lessons of your own choosing. The Test Generator also allows you to construct alternative forms of a test to preserve test security and/or for test–retest purposes. You may also prepare pre- and post-tests as a basis for differentiating instruction and as a means of documenting learning gains for individual students or for the whole class.

Endnotes

[1] Stahl, 3; Southwest Educational Development Laboratory, 14.

[2] Biemiller, 24.

[3] Stahl, 9; Texas Reading Initiative, 5–6.

[4] Stahl, 30.

[5] Stahl, 30; Texas Reading Initiative, 20.

[6] Texas Reading Initiative, 8.

[7] Hunt and Beglar, 1.

[8] Stahl, 15.

[9] Stahl, 31–32; Texas Reading Initiative, 21–23.

[10] Biemiller, 28.

[11] Stahl, 12.

[12] Texas Reading Initiative, 14.

[13] Texas Reading Initiative, 19.

[14] Stahl, 11 and 28–29.

[15] Texas Reading Initiative, 20.

[16] Stahl, 29.

[17] Biemiller, 28.

[18] Texas Reading Initiative, 40.

[19] Stahl and Nagy, 164.

[20] Texas Reading Initiative, 36–38.

[21] Stahl, 45.

[22] Texas Reading Initiative, 28; Stahl, 43.

[23] This section is adapted from Stahl, 37–39, and Texas Reading Initiative, 30 and 31.

[24] Stahl, 39–40; Texas Reading Initiative, 32–33.

[25] Southwest Educational Development Laboratory, 14.

[26] Stahl, 13.

[27] Stahl, 34.

Bibliography

Biemiller, Andrew. "Teaching Vocabulary: Early, Direct, and Sequential." *American Educator.* Spring 2001.

Hunt, Alan, and David Beglar. "Current Research and Practice in Teaching Vocabulary." *The Language Teacher Online,* 22.01 (January 1998). Online. Available at <http://langue.hyper.chubu.ac.jp/jalt/pub/tlt/98/jan/hunt.html>. Accessed March 15, 2003.

Southwest Educational Development Laboratory. "The Cognitive Foundations of Learning to Read: A Framework." Online. Available at <http://www.sedl.org/reading/framework/framework.pdf>. Accessed March 15, 2003.

Stahl, Steven A. *Vocabulary Development.* Cambridge, MA: Brookline Books, 1999.

Stahl, Steven A. and William E. Nagy. *Teaching Word Meanings.* Mahwah, N.J.: Lawrence Erlbaum Associates, 2006.

Texas Reading Initiative/Texas Education Agency. *Promoting Vocabulary Development.* Austin, TX: Texas Reading Initiative/Texas Education Agency, 2000.

Student Book Answer Key

Lesson 1

1A Finding Meanings p. 3
1. b—d
2. d—b
3. c—b
4. b—c
5. b—c
6. c—d
7. c—a
8. b—d
9. d—a

1B Just the Right Word p. 4
1. lack
2. developed
3. projects
4. ease
5. complete
6. mastered
7. represents
8. benefit
9. patriotism
10. dismayed
11. recommended

1C Applying Meanings p. 4
1. a, c
2. a, c, d
3. b, c, d
4. a, b
5. b, c, d
6. c, d
7. a
8. a, d

1D Word Study p. 5
1. benefit, help
2. finish, complete
3. develop, grow
4. alarm, dismay
5. ease, comfort
6. hail, greet
7. shortage, lack
8. suggest, recommend
9. comment, remark
10. utter, say

1E Passage p. 6
(The appropriate vocabulary word is printed in boldface. Sentences are examples; students' sentences may vary.)
1. He loved his people, worked for them, and had their best interests a heart.
2. *Utter* means "to speak."
3. There were no books written in Cherokee before 1821 because th Cherokees **lacked** a written language.
4. Sequoya was **dismayed** at what the white settlers were doing.
5. *Develop* means "to bring into being."
6. He used the letters of these alphabets to **represent** syllables in th Cherokee language.
7. The Cherokees had eighty-six sounds to represent.
8. His work took twelve years to **complete**.
9. He worked on the project with his daughter.
10. It was popular because they could learn it with **ease**.
11. We can tell the Cherokee leaders liked the new system because the **recommended** that it be taught to everyone who wanted to learn t read and write.
12. *Hailed* means "welcomed with enthusiasm and admiration."
13. Those who **mastered** it taught others.
14. He was a silversmith, a painter, and a soldier, as well as the inventor the Cherokee alphabet.
15. A written language enables people living apart to communicate wit each other by letter.

Lesson 2

2A Finding Meanings p. 10
1. c—b
2. c—d
3. a—d
4. b—d
5. d—b
6. a—b
7. a—d
8. c—a
9. b—c
10. d—a

2B Just the Right Word p. 11
1. column
2. exceeds
3. calculate
4. affect
5. mature
6. climate
7. forbid
8. resist
9. decay
10. scorching

2C Applying Meanings p. 12
1. a, c
2. a, b, c
3. b
4. c, d
5. a, b, d
6. a, b
7. a, b
8. a, b, c

2D Word Study p. 13
1. develop, decay
2. permit, forbid
3. difficulty, ease
4. resist, surrender
5. start, complete
6. harm, benefit
7. mammoth, tiny
8. joy, dismay
9. childish, mature
10. lack, excess

2E Passage p. 14
1. Forest fires **scorch** their outside bark.
2. You can find them in Redwood National Park, in northwest California
3. You cannot cut down a redwood tree in California because it is **forbidden**.
4. The lowest **limbs** can be 150 feet above the ground.
5. The trunks of redwoods look like **columns** of a Greek temple.
6. The oldest sequoia and redwood trees can **exceed** three thousan years.
7. *Towering* is a good word because the trees are as tall as towers.
8. Their bark is thickest when they are **matured**.
9. Thick bark helps them **resist** disease.
10. California does not **permit** you to cut down a sequoia.
11. Redwood is used because it does not **decay** as quickly as other wood
12. Sequoias don't grow along the coast because they need the colde drier **climate** inland.
13. The **mammoth** General Grant trees' trunk is almost a hundred fe around.
14. It has been **calculated** that a full-grown sequoia contains enough woo to build thirty houses.
15. They have lived so long because they are not **affected** by fire and di ease the way other trees are.

Lesson 3

3A Finding Meanings p. 18
1. d—a
2. c—d
3. b—c
4. a—b
5. b—c
6. c—b
7. a—b
8. d—a
9. c—b
10. a—d

3B Just the Right Word p. 19
1. drowsy
2. cease
3. hibernate
4. nestled
5. approaches
6. migration
7. severe
8. reduction
9. burrowed
10. observed

3C Applying Meanings p. 20
1. a, d
2. b
3. b, d
4. a, b, c, d
5. a, b, d
6. a, b, d
7. a, b, c, d
8. a, b, c

3D Word Study p. 21
1. *propius*, near
2. *hibernus*, winter
3. *fames*, hunger
4. *plere*, complete
5. *cessare*, stop
6. *servare*, watch
7. *severus*, strict
8. *jacere*, throw
9. *bene*, well
10. *calculus*, pebble

3E Passage p. 22
1. Woodchucks **hibernate** in winter.
2. A woodchuck makes a nest and closes off openings of the tunnels th lead to it.
3. The woodchuck becomes so fat it can hardly move.
4. Before it begins its long sleep, it starts to feel **drowsy**.
5. They keep from freezing by sleeping in a **burrow** deep underground
6. The temperature might be below zero in a severe winter.
7. It needs only a little oxygen because its breathing almost **ceases**.
8. It **nestles** in its underground bed.
9. The woodchuck's size is **reduced** to only half of what it was in the fa
10. *Observe* means "to notice."
11. It is famished because it hasn't eaten all winter.
12. He could **forecast** the weather.
13. The woodchuck **ventures** above ground; if he sees his shadow, it mea winter is not over, and he goes back to sleep.
14. Many northern birds **migrate** south in the fall and return in th spring.
15. Woodchucks eat garden plants during the summer.

Wordly Wise 3000 Book

Lesson 4

A Finding Meanings   p. 27
1. b—a
2. a—d
3. b—a
4. a—c
5. b—a
6. a—d
7. b—d
8. b—c
9. d—a
10. c—d
11. a—c

B Just the Right Word   p. 28
1. exposed
2. astound
3. modesty
4. paralyzed
5. grace
6. active
7. pessimist
8. imposing
9. contracts
10. attend

4C Applying Meanings   p. 28
1. a, b, c
2. a, b, c
3. a, b, c
4. a, b
5. a, b, c
6. b, c
7. a
8. b, c, d

4D Word Study   p. 29
1. astound, amaze
2. observe, notice
3. mammoth, huge
4. eager, willing
5. cherish, love
6. pessimistic, hopeful
7. drowsy, active
8. boastful, modest
9. expose, hide
10. enlarge, reduce

4E Passage   p. 31
1. It wasn't until she was eight that the family had saved enough money from their **modest** income.
2. She was **paralyzed** and could neither run nor walk.
3. They were **pessimistic** about her living more than a year or two.
4. They get very sick, and their muscles are affected.
5. *Active* means "lively; moving around a lot."
6. The narrative says he **cherished** her.
7. He was surprised that she was able to walk as well as she did.
8. Her movements were jerky.
9. She was **eager** to go to school.
10. *Attend* means "to go to."
11. They begin at a certain distance apart and that distance remains the same no matter how far they are extended.
12. They probably didn't want their citizens to learn about conditions in their countries or foreigners to learn about conditions in China.
13. She gave **recitals** for visitors.
14. The person probably expected her either to stay at home or to use a wheelchair.
15. She might have left the stage.

Lesson 5

A Finding Meanings   p. 35
1. d—a
2. a—b
3. c—b
4. b—c
5. d—a
6. d—c
7. a—b
8. b—c
9. c—b
10. a—c

B Just the Right Word   p. 36
1. sensitive
2. quaint
3. abrupt
4. achieve
5. entertained
6. persists
7. mocked
8. glimpsed
9. revise
10. phase

5C Applying Meanings   p. 37
1. b, c, d
2. b, c, d
3. a, b
4. a, b, c, d
5. b, c, d
6. b, c, d
7. a, c, d
8. a, b

5D Word Study   p. 38
1. unpatriotic
2. unremarkable
3. immature
4. unaffected
5. insufficient
6. incomplete
7. undeveloped
8. unpersuasive
9. immodest
10. insensitive
11. inactive
12. unprepared

5E Passage   p. 39
1. He might have turned inward.
2. He **entertained** his parents by putting on plays.
3. They were dressed in **quaint** clothes that he made.
4. His father died when he was eleven.
5. He might have told her he would be happier there and might find work.
6. He failed at every job he **attempted**.
7. They treated him with **contempt**.
8. No. His plays were **rejected**.
9. He tried acting, dancing, singing, and writing plays.
10. His fairy tales were his greatest achievement.
11. He **recalled** the stories his father told him when he was little.
12. He **revised** his sentences until he got them just right.
13. He was **persistent**.
14. He was different—a daydreamer and an artist.
15. It gives his readers a **glimpse** into the author's life.

Lesson 6

A Finding Meanings   p. 43
1. b—a
2. c—b
3. c—a
4. b—d
5. d—b
6. a—d
7. a—c
8. c—d
9. a—b
10. c—d
11. c—d

B Just the Right Word   p. 44
1. peered
2. in vain
3. refined
4. jeers
5. progress
6. exclaimed
7. crafty
8. disclose
9. applause

6C Applying Meanings   p. 45
1. a
2. a, d
3. a, b
4. a, d
5. a, b
6. b, c, d
7. a, c
8. a, c, d

6D Word Study   p. 46
1. recall, remember
2. uneasy, nervous
3. disclose, reveal
4. jeer, mock
5. abrupt, sudden
6. vain, modest
7. exquisite, drab
8. crafty, foolish
9. contempt, respect
10. applaud, jeer

6E Passage   p. 47
1. He spent hours **peering** at himself in the mirror.
2. They told him the new clothes would make the old ones seem **drab**.
3. *Refined* taste is sensitive and thoughtful.
4. It was impossible because they were just pretending and weren't really working.
5. They were scoundrels because they were dishonest and were tricking the emperor.
6. A child in the crowd shouted out the truth.
7. They were uneasy because they were lying to the emperor.
8. They told him his new clothes were the most **exquisite** they'd ever seen.
9. They probably thought they were very **crafty**.
10. They wanted to make him appear ridiculous and show people how vain he was.
11. They were pretending to admire his "new clothes."
12. The child was telling the truth and describing what the crowd actually saw.
13. Palace officers made sure everyone turned out to see him.
14. He ran back because the crowd was **jeering** at him.
15. **Vain** describes him perfectly because it means that he had much too high an opinion of himself and his appearance.

Lesson 7

7A Finding Meanings   p. 51
1. a—d   5. d—c   8. b—a
2. c—b   6. a—b   9. a—d
3. b—c   7. c—b   10. c—b
4. a—d

7B Just the Right Word   p. 52
1. limp
2. embraced
3. shallow
4. scurried
5. instant
6. confusing
7. alteration
8. distributed
9. surrounded
10. ejected

7C Applying Meanings   p. 53
1. a, c   5. a, d
2. b, c, d   6. a, b
3. a, b, d   7. c, d
4. a, b   8. b, d

7D Word Study   p. 54
1. re-, against
2. ex-, out
3. pre-, before
4. un-, not
5. re-, again
6. ex-, out
7. re-, again
8. ex-, out
9. e-, out
10. re-, again

7E Passage   p. 5
1. It changes its color to match its **surroundings**.
2. It can change colors in an **instant**.
3. It makes a "screen" to **confuse** an attacker.
4. It **ejects** a blob of black, ink-like liquid.
5. It makes it easy for it to **alter** its shape.
6. If they had bones, the octopus's arms would be less **flexible**.
7. It has two rows of deeply set suckers that give it a powerful grip.
8. Its arms help it to **seize** animals that go by.
9. A crab would start scurrying because it could easily be seized by the octopus's arms.
10. It uses its beaks to crack the shell of its **victim**.
11. Its eyesight is very **keen**.
12. They are **distributed** throughout the world's oceans.
13. They live mostly in warm, **shallow** water.
14. No. If you don't struggle, but remain relaxed, the octopus will let you go.
15. *Limp* means "not stiff, but relaxed."

Lesson 8

8A Finding Meanings   p. 59
1. a—b   5. b—c   8. b—c
2. b—c   6. c—a   9. d—b
3. d—c   7. d—a   10. b—c
4. a—d

8B Just the Right Word   p. 60
1. spacious
2. century
3. location
4. ramp
5. quarry
6. entry
7. portion
8. chambers
9. passage
10. surfaced

8C Applying Meanings   p. 61
1. a, b, c   5. b, c
2. c, d   6. a, c, d
3. c   7. a, c
4. a, b, c   8. b, c, d

8D Word Study   p. 62
1. roomy
2. valuable
3. eager
4. old
5. cheer
6. find
7. change
8. grasp
9. hug
10. improve

8E Passage   p. 6
1. It is the only **ancient** sight that remains today.
2. One goes through **passages** connecting the rooms.
3. The rooms in the interior must not have had windows on the outsi and so did not get any light.
4. They dragged them up a **ramp** of earth.
5. It had to come by water since it came from **quarries** near the N River.
6. The people who worked only a portion of the year were farmer whose fields were flooded at that time, and so could not farm.
7. It was one of the most **spacious** rooms.
8. *Chamber* is another word for *room*.
9. Jewels and objects made of gold might have been left with the de king.
10. The Egyptians put granite slabs outside the tomb to keep people fro gaining **entry** to it.
11. **Intruders** stole the gold and the jewels.
12. The Great Pyramid was built more than 20 **centuries** ago.
13. They believed he was a god, a descendant of the sun god, Ra.
14. At first its **surface** was smooth white limestone, but most of this is no gone.
15. Cairo is in Egypt.

Lesson 9

9A Finding Meanings   p. 68
1. a—b   5. a—c   8. a—b
2. b—a   6. c—d   9. c—a
3. d—c   7. d—a   10. c—b
4. b—d

9B Just the Right Word   p. 69
1. distance
2. parched
3. advantage
4. sole
5. shrewd
6. founder
7. scare
8. typical
9. host
10. tormenting

9C Applying Meanings   p. 70
1. a   6. a, b
2. b, c, d   7. a, b, c
3. b, c, d   8. b, c
4. a, b, d   9. a, b, c, d
5. a, b   10. c

9D Word Study   p. 71
1. alteration
2. confusion
3. response
4. exclamation
5. intention
6. persistence
7. migration
8. paralysis
9. excess
10. preparation
11. applause
12. location

9E Passage   p. 7
1. They were known as the forty-niners.
2. They sold them water at very high prices.
3. The businessmen wanted to get rich quickly.
4. Water was very scarce in the desert.
5. No, the **typical** person only earned about a dollar a day.
6. They might have suffered from hunger and thirst, as well as heat.
7. No, San Francisco was just a tiny **hamlet**.
8. People might have been worried about leaving their families and the jobs and taking a risk that they would find gold.
9. Sam Brannan was one of the **founders** of San Francisco.
10. He bought up pick axes, shovels, and pans so he could sell them for high price.
11. President James Polk made it known that gold had been discovered.
12. It was over 17,000 miles.
13. The growth of San Francisco was **astonishing**.
14. They are called **prospectors**.
15. Only newspapers gave this kind of information.

Wordly Wise 3000 Book

Lesson 10

10A Finding Meanings   p. 76

1. b—c
2. d—c
3. a—b
4. d—b
5. c—b
6. b—c
7. b—c
8. c—b
9. b—c
10. c—b

10B Just the Right Word   p. 77

1. deliberated
2. misfortune
3. slay
4. ails
5. desire
6. precipice
7. cower
8. consolation
9. orphans
10. banish
11. depths

10C Applying Meanings   p. 78

1. a, b, d
2. a, b, d
3. b, d
4. a
5. b, c
6. b, c
7. a, b, c, d
8. b, c, d

10D Word Study   p. 79

1. *project*, verb
2. *project*, noun
3. *permit*, noun
4. *permit*, verb
5. *contract*, noun
6. *contract*, verb
7. *reject*, noun
8. *reject*, verb
9. *progress*, verb
10. *progress*, noun

10E Passage   p. 80

1. Tokoyo and her father were reunited, and her father **regained** his freedom.
2. No. She had a father.
3. *Misfortune struck* means "terrible things happened suddenly."
4. The sea god had cast a spell on him, causing many **ailments**.
5. They tried to **console** her and lift her spirits.
6. He lived in the **depths** of the sea.
7. She searched for him, and had her knife ready so she could attack him.
8. **Communication** between father and daughter was forbidden.
9. He was **banished** to the island because he made a joke about the emperor.
10. She went to the island because she had a strong **desire** to see her father.
11. She was about to be thrown into the sea as a sacrifice to the sea god.
12. She was **cowering** in fear.
13. She wanted to get to the bottom of the sea so she could **slay** the sea god.
14. All his **symptoms** disappeared.
15. Diving for oysters was their **livelihood**. They were searching for pearls.

Lesson 11

11A Finding Meanings   p. 84

1. b—a
2. c—d
3. c—d
4. d—c
5. a—c
6. a—c
7. a—b
8. a—b
9. b—a
10. b—c
11. b—c

11B Just the Right Word   p. 86

1. yield
2. annual
3. boring
4. evaporates
5. nourishes
6. crude
7. blending
8. hues
9. vision
10. artificial

11C Applying Meanings   p. 86

1. b, c
2. c, d
3. b, c
4. a, b, d
5. a, c, d
6. a, b
7. a, d
8. c, d

11D Word Study   p. 87

1. lessen
2. rise
3. slight
4. new
5. cramped
6. natural
7. lose
8. upset
9. worthless
10. refined

11E Passage   p. 88

1. The syrup is a **blend** of cane sugar syrup and real maple syrup.
2. Cane sugar syrup is cheaper and more plentiful than real maple syrup.
3. Another word for the leaves of a tree is **foliage**.
4. Maple trees are a visual treat in the late fall.
5. You might see brilliant reds and golds.
6. The amount **varies** between twelve and twenty gallons.
7. *Yield* means "to produce."
8. Sap **nourishes** the trees.
9. On sunny days, the flow of sap **increases**.
10. They needed axes to make **gashes** in the trees.
11. This method could cause **considerable** damage to the tree.
12. In order to get at the syrup, tree farmers **bore** holes in the trunk.
13. That syrup is **crude**, and needs to be refined before it is ready to use.
14. When it is boiled, the water in it **evaporates**.
15. Maple sugaring occurs **annually**.

Lesson 12

12A Finding Meanings   p. 92

1. a—d
2. d—b
3. d—c
4. c—b
5. a—c
6. c—b
7. c—b
8. b—c
9. d—a
10. b—d

12B Just the Right Word   p. 93

1. separated
2. gestured
3. request
4. recovery
5. moped
6. clutch
7. replace
8. ability
9. furious
10. bliss

12C Applying Meanings   p. 94

1. b, d
2. a, b, c
3. b, c
4. a, c
5. b, c
6. b, c, d
7. a, b
8. a, b

12D Word Study   p. 95

1. ask
2. request
3. avoid
4. shun
5. slay
6. kill
7. wish
8. desire
9. happiness
10. bliss
11. ancient
12. old
13. change
14. alter

12E Passage   p. 97

1. *Gesture* means "movement of the hand."
2. She became ill and had to be **separated** from the other gorillas.
3. She preferred books with pictures of gorillas and cats.
4. She gave her a cat because Koko **requested** it.
5. Koko had an **amiable** personality.
6. *Furious* means "very angry."
7. She could not be coaxed, and refused to play with the toy cat.
8. She shunned it because she knew it wasn't real, and she wanted a real one.
9. She picked it up and **caressed** it.
10. All Ball **clutched** Koko's fur.
11. She **moped** for days afterward.
12. *Replace* means "to take the place of."
13. She **recovered** her good spirits.
14. It gave her the **ability** to make jokes.
15. You would feel totally, completely happy.

Lesson 13

13A Finding Meanings p. 104
1. d—b
2. b—d
3. a—b
4. d—a
5. b—d
6. d—c
7. d—b
8. d—b
9. a—b
10. d—b

13B Just the Right Word p. 105
1. depend
2. dreary
3. isolated
4. temporary
5. appalled
6. invaded
7. suspects
8. terror
9. routed
10. tragedies

13C Applying Meanings p. 105
1. a, b
2. a, b, c, d
3. b, d
4. c, d
5. b, c, d
6. a, c, d
7. a, b, c, d
8. a, b, d

13D Word Study p. 106
1. *solus*, alone
2. *rumpere*, to break
3. *visus*, to see
4. *centum*, hundred
5. *tempus*, time
6. *visus*, to see
7. *amicus*, friend
8. *annus*, year
9. *locus*, place
10. *jacere*, to throw

13E Passage p. 10
1. Answers will vary.
2. Hitler's armies **invaded** their country.
3. He intended to murder all the Jews in all the countries he could.
4. He had a **fanatic** hatred of Jews.
5. They lived in **terror** that the Germans would round them up and tak them away.
6. *Occupied* means "lived in."
7. They **depended** on friends to bring them food.
8. They hoped Hitler would be defeated.
9. Answers will vary.
10. She **revealed** the details of her life in hiding as well as her feelings; sh was the same age as many of her readers.
11. They had no contact with the outside world and were closeted in a tin space.
12. She must have been most dejected when the Nazis rounded up he family and when their hiding place was discovered.
13. No one **suspected** that they were hiding behind the bookshelf.
14. His armies were **routed** by the Russians, Americans, and British.
15. Answers will vary.

Lesson 14

14A Finding Meanings p. 111
1. b—c
2. d—a
3. a—b
4. b—c
5. c—a
6. a—d
7. a—d
8. c—a
9. c—a
10. a—d

14B Just the Right Word p. 112
1. submit
2. plead
3. humble
4. boast
5. relented
6. trudged
7. plunged
8. fringe
9. afford
10. melancholy

14C Applying Meanings p. 113
1. c
2. a, b, c, d
3. a, b, c
4. a, d
5. a, b, c
6. a, b, c
7. a, b, c
8. a, b, c

14D Word Study p. 114
1. dependable
2. variable
3. remarkable
4. preferable
5. affordable
6. desirable
7. entertainment
8. replacement
9. nourishment
10. equipment
11. achievement
12. resentment

14E Passage p. 11
1. They grew along the **fringes** of the lake.
2. The music became very **melancholy**.
3. *Afford* means "to be able to pay for."
4. They lived in a **humble** cottage.
5. She **boasted** to her neighbors about the silver cows.
6. They went up the mountain to a **meadow** by the side of the lake.
7. They seemed to be responding to the **chords** he played on his harp.
8. It was an **exceptional** quality.
9. She felt fortunate because the silver cows gave twice as much milk a the black and white ones.
10. When his mother told him to be quiet, he **submitted** to her will.
11. He **pleaded** with her to spare the animal.
12. No. She would not **relent**.
13. *Trudged* suggests he was sad and heavy-hearted.
14. She was a very **obstinate** person.
15. He last saw the silver cows when they ran to the edge of the lake an **plunged** in.

Lesson 15

15A Finding Meanings p. 119
1. d—a
2. a—d
3. a—c
4. a—d
5. b—a
6. d—c
7. b—c
8. b—a
9. c—a
10. c—b
11. b—c

15B Just the Right Word p. 121
1. fragile
2. pounced
3. prompted
4. talons
5. trophy
6. contrasts
7. Concentrate
8. considered
9. concerns

15C Applying Meanings p. 121
1. a, c
2. b
3. a, b, c, d
4. a, b
5. b, c
6. a, b, c, d
7. b, c
8. a, b, d

15D Word Study p. 122
1. *con*, with
2. *con*, together
3. *com*, with
4. *com*, with
5. *con*, with
6. *con*, with
7. *con*, with
8. *con*, together
9. *com*, with
10. *con*, with

15E Passage p. 12
1. A farmer would be most likely to kill a bald eagle when he/she sees i with a small animal in its **talons**.
2. It became **apparent** in the 1950s.
3. Their eggs were **fragile** and when they broke, the chicks inside wer killed.
4. The number of bald eagles has been increasing in **recent** years.
5. Human beings are the only creatures that **menace** the bald eagle.
6. It **pounces** on small animals and fish.
7. She wrote *Silent Spring*, a book about the damage some chemical were doing to wildlife.
8. It became **concentrated** in lakes and streams.
9. It was in **widespread** use in the United States.
10. They had them stuffed as **trophies.**
11. *Considered* means "seriously thought to be."
12. It was important because there was a big drop in the bald eagl population.
13. Congress passed a law **banning** the use of DDT.
14. It got its name from its white-feathered head, which **contrasts** with it brown-feathered body.
15. It is a **symbol** of America.

Lesson 16

16A Finding Meanings   p. 127
1. b—c   4. d—b   7. c—d
2. b—d   5. d—b   8. c—b
3. a—c   6. b—c   9. d—a

16B Just the Right Word   p. 128
1. detest
2. bough
3. content
4. wander
5. orchard
6. threadbare
7. practicing
8. apt
9. obtain
10. familiar
11. blossom

16C Applying Meanings   p. 129
1. a, b, c   5. a, d
2. a   6. a, b
3. a, b   7. a, b, c, d
4. a, c   8. b, c

16D Word Study   p. 130
1. quick
2. forbid
3. hate
4. beg
5. shabby
6. stubborn
7. lucky
8. get
9. danger
10. satisfied
11. modest
12. sad

16E Passage   p. 131
1. It's an apt name because he planted apple seeds as he traveled.
2. As a result of his planting, **orchards** were growing wherever he had visited.
3. His clothes were **threadbare**, but that did not bother him.
4. He **detested** killing of any kind.
5. As he traveled, he usually just **wandered** from one place to another.
6. *Practice* means "something that he usually did."
7. He **obtained** them from cider mills in New England.
8. He looked for a **stout** bough of an apple tree.
9. At **dusk**, he looked for a place to spend the night.
10. He was **content** to sleep outside.
11. He once **extinguished** his campfire because it was attracting mosquitoes, who were killed by the flames.
12. He loved the sight of **blossoms** on the apple trees.
13. The **boughs** of the trees were full of fruit.
14. He was a **familiar** sight to people who lived in the Ohio River Valley.
15. He would return so he could **prune** the trees to make sure they stayed healthy.

Lesson 17

17A Finding Meanings   p. 136
1. b—d   5. d—b   8. a—d
2. d—a   6. b—a   9. d—c
3. d—a   7. c—b   10. b—c
4. a—d

17B Just the Right Word   p. 137
1. wafted
2. deprived
3. fare
4. conclusion
5. escort
6. approval
7. hearty
8. stingy
9. merits
10. addressed

17C Applying Meanings   p. 138
1. a, b, c, d   5. b
2. a, b   6. a, b, c, d
3. a, b, d   7. a, b, c, d
4. b, c   8. a, c

17D Word Study   p. 139
1. hail
2. hale
3. pier
4. peer
5. vein
6. vain
7. slay
8. sleigh
9. bore
10. boar
11. fare
12. fair
13. chord
14. cord
15. bough
16. bow

17E Passage   p. 141
1. No. He was shy and afraid to speak.
2. *Hearty* means "satisfying."
3. Instead of giving his leftover food to needy families, he gave it to his pigs.
4. The *tajiri* did not get what he wanted—the goat. He was granted only the "right to smell the goat."
5. The smells of delicious food would not have **wafted** out.
6. He saw the *maskini* **inhale** deeply and look blissful.
7. He needed an escort because he probably wouldn't have gone to jail willingly.
8. Yes, he was **summoned** before the court.
9. It would be decided on the basis of the facts of the case.
10. The *tajiri* claimed the *maskini* was **depriving** him of the smells from the kitchen.
11. He was probably terrified of losing his goat.
12. An older person whom other villagers respected might become an **elder**.
13. The chief **addressed** the crowd near the court.
14. *Concluded* means "formed an opinion."
15. They might have applauded.

Lesson 18

18A Word Meanings   p. 144
1. c—b   5. d—a   9. a—b
2. a—d   6. d—a   10. c—b
3. c—d   7. d—b   11. c—a
4. c—a   8. b—c

18B Just the Right Word   p. 145
1. utilizes
2. fortress
3. capital
4. petty
5. threaten
6. frequent
7. abreast
8. vast
9. external
10. frontiers
11. feud

18C Applying Meanings   p. 146
1. a, c, d   5. a, b, c, d
2. c, d   6. a, b, c
3. b, d   7. a, c
4. b, c   8. b

18D Word Study   p. 147
1. generous
2. strange
3. reject
4. fragile
5. rare
6. light
7. resist
8. start
9. exciting
10. cowardly
11. tiny
12. blissful

18E Passage   p. 148
1. They visit it because it is one of the most famous sights in China.
2. It takes a long time because it is such a **vast** country.
3. Beijing is the **capital** of China.
4. It was built as a **barrier** against tribes from the north.
5. He worried about **external** attacks.
6. They spent most of their time **feuding**.
7. He might have influence only over that small kingdom.
8. Those tribes were **threatening** his rule.
9. It would have taken place on China's northern **frontier**.
10. They **utilized** whatever was close at hand.
11. They housed the emperor's soldiers.
12. The top was so wide ten people could walk **abreast**.
13. The **breadth** of the wall is nearly twenty feet.
14. They were forced to leave their farms and had to carry everything either on their backs or slung on poles.
15. Yes, it **ensured** the safety of Shi Huang-ti's empire by protecting it from outside attacks.

Lesson 19

19A Finding Meanings   p. 152

1. c—d
2. b—a
3. b—a
4. a—d
5. b—c
6. d—a
7. a—d
8. b—c
9. d—a

19B Just the Right Word   p. 153

1. foremost
2. trio
3. source
4. eliminate
5. engaged
6. elevate
7. sentimental
8. created
9. recognize
10. auditions
11. entrancing

19C Applying Meanings   p. 154

1. a, c
2. a
3. a, b, c
4. b, d
5. a, b, c
6. a, d
7. a, c
8. c

19D Word Study   p. 155

1. triangle
2. trillion
3. triplets
4. trial
5. tricycle
6. trident
7. tricolor
8. trio
9. tribe
10. triplicate
11. tripod
12. trickle

19E Passage   p. 15

1. Dance companies go on **tour** around the country.
2. She **eliminated** things she felt were unnecessary.
3. They had tight waists, short skirts, tights, and stiffened ballet shoes.
4. It was a stage that was stripped to its **essentials**, with bare stage settings and simple costumes.
5. They were based on **sentimental** stories and followed fixed patterns of movement.
6. She used a variety of **sources**, including Native American life, scenes from American history, and the poetry of Emily Dickinson.
7. She was **entranced** by her work.
8. She wanted to concentrate on teaching and developing her own style of dancing.
9. *Engage* means "to hire."
10. She needed two others.
11. *Recognized* means "accepted and approved."
12. At the time of her death, she was **creating** a new dance for her company.
13. She **elevated** modern dance to a new American art form.
14. She was one of the **foremost** dancers of the twentieth century.
15. You have to **audition**.

Lesson 20

20A Finding Meanings   p. 160

1. a—d
2. a—d
3. c—a
4. d—c
5. a—c
6. d—b
7. c—b
8. c—a
9. d—a
10. b—c

20B Just the Right Word   p. 161

1. pierced
2. eventually
3. implored
4. sullen
5. inserted
6. disputed
7. congratulations
8. humiliation
9. helm
10. capable
11. despise

20C Applying Meanings   p. 162

1. a, b
2. a, b, c, d
3. b, c, d
4. c
5. a, d
6. a, c
7. a, b, d
8. a, c

20D Word Study   p. 163

1. arrest, stop   S
2. despise, cherish   A
3. valiant, fearless   S
4. quarrel, feud   S
5. astonish, astound   S
6. sullen, amiable,   A
7. yield, resist,   A
8. banish, welcome   A
9. remember, recall   S
10. lower, elevate   A
11. beg, implore   S
12. forlorn, sad   S
13. create, destroy   A
14. capture, release   A
15. eliminate, remove   S

20E Passage   p. 16

1. Yes. His "crime" was refusing to bow before the cap on the pole.
2. Although they obeyed the order, they were **sullen**.
3. The cap was a symbol of Austrian rule.
4. They don't believe he really existed.
5. Gessler **despised** the Swiss people.
6. He ordered him to jail because he was **outraged** when Tell told him he would have killed him if his son had been hurt.
7. He didn't think they were **capable** of ruling themselves.
8. They were waiting for him to **release** the arrow.
9. He **inserted** the first one in his crossbow and the second in his belt.
10. *Quiver* means "a case for holding arrows."
11. He intended to **pierce** Gessler's heart.
12. He **congratulated** William Tell for demonstrating such skill.
13. The crew cowered below.
14. They **implored** William Tell to take over.
15. No, but it **eventually** led to Swiss freedom from Austrian rule.

Lessons 1–4
Crossword Puzzle

```
C O M P L E T E       V           D E C A Y
  A         A T T E N D       D   X   L
U T T E R   R   G       N O       O C E A N
  U     E A S E       T W O       E   M
A R M     R           D E V E L O P       P
P R E P A R E     E                   P   A
P     R   G R O V E     E           P R   R
R   P K   G           A C H E   A       A L
A   A     N   S C O R C H     L   R
A C T I V E   O       O     D I S M A Y
C   R   S     L       L     M   I   S
H A I L   T   B U R R O W   A   T   I
  O   L   M       R     T       S
  T O W E R I N G     S E V E R E
```

page 33

Lessons 5–8
Crossword Puzzle

```
D I S T R I B U T E     P E R S U A D E
  U   E       N   E     H   B
  R   C     A L T E R   Q U A R R Y
S U R F A C E     E   S     T   U
  O   L     P O R T I O N     P
D O U B L E   T   S     E N T R Y
E   N   M   C R A F T Y   Y
  D R A B     I       E V E       S
  E     R E F I N E   E   S   S E I Z E
  J   A       J       K       V
N I N E   C H A M B E R   E N T I R E
D   C   E         C     E         R
  T     L O C A T I O N
```

page 66

Lessons 9–12
Hidden Message

```
D I S T A N C E
G A S H
H A M L E T
    T O R M E N T
S O L E
```

```
P R E C I P I C E
C O N S O L E
```

```
A N N U A L
```

```
R E G A I N
S C A R C E
S H R E W D
A D V A N T A G E
A S T O N I S H
```

```
C R U D E
I N C R E A S E
    B A N I S H
A B I L I T Y
```

```
E V A P O R A T E
C O N F I R M
```

```
S Y M P T O M
L I V E L I H O O D
C A R E S S
C O A X
    S L A Y
A N N U A L
S E P A R A T E
R E Q U E S T S
```

```
D E P T H
M I S F O R T U N E
```

```
D E L I B E R A T E
A I L M E N T
```

```
F O L I A G E
  A M I A B L E
  F U R I O U S
  F O U N D E R S
    H U E
B L E N D
```

```
A R T I F I C I A L
  V A R Y
R E C O V E R
    M O P E
```

```
C L U T C H
G E S T U R E D
B O R E
    B L I S S   .
P R E F E R
H O S T
    S H U N
```

```
            K
C O M M U N I C A T E
    P R O S P E C T
    C O W E R
R E P L A C E
    Y I E L D
        D E S I R E
    M I S G I V I N G S
P A R C H E D
```

pages 99–101

Lessons 13–16
Crossword Puzzle

```
R O U T . . . S U S P E C T . I . I
. B . R . . . T . . . O . B O A S T
. T . O . C H O R D . . S . . W . O
. A L P . L . U . . . S . T A B L E
. I . H . E X T I N G U I S H . . A
A N D Y . A . . . . . D . R . . . T
. R . . . N . C . D E J E C T E . D
P L E A D . T A L O N . R . A . R E
R . A . P . R . N . B . D . A P T .
O . R . R . R . T W O . B . G . E .
M A Y . H U M B L E . U . A . I . S
P . . . N . I . N . G . R . C . T .
T R U D G E . A . T . H O N E Y . .
```

page 134

Lessons 17–20
Crossword Puzzle

```
E S C O R T . A P P R O V E . . . A
. O . R . Q . O . L O W E R . . . R
C O N G R A T U L A T E . D . E . R
. C . D . I . A . E L E V A T E . S
. L . I . V A S T . . R . P . . . T
F E U D . T . E . O . B . O . . . T
O . D . P I E R C E P E A S A N T .
R . E . O . . . S . R . . . . . . I
T . M . N . . U . R . . . P E N . S
R . E . A . H U M I L I A T E . . .
E N T R A N C E . M . E . T . . . E
S . I . H . O . R . T . . . . . . R
S . T H R E A T E N . E G Y P T . .
```

page 167

Lesson Review Exercises

Lesson 1

1. White people kept taking over more and more of the land that belonged to the Cherokees. They felt that they did not have _____ land for their needs.

2. Sequoya wanted the Cherokees to take pride in their past. He showed his _____ by giving them a way to record the history of their nation.

3. The difference between spoken and written language is that written words are read, while spoken words are _____.

4. Sequoya is remembered today mainly for one thing. He is the only person in history to have invented a _____ alphabet.

5. Sequoya enjoyed working with his hands as well as his mind. He took pride in whatever he did, whether as a painter or as a _____ silversmith.

6. Sequoya invented the written Cherokee language with his daughter's help. The two of them _____ the language over a twelve-year period.

7. Sequoya hoped that the Cherokee leaders would believe in what he was doing. He would have been _____ if they had turned down his idea.

8. Sequoya showed his invention to the Cherokee leaders. They told him to go ahead with his _____.

9. The Cherokee alphabet is different from the English one. In English, some of the letters _____ more than one sound.

10. The Cherokee leaders were impressed with Sequoya's invention. They _____ it as a great step forward for their people.

11. The Cherokee people were able to learn to read and write quite easily. Sequoya's system was _____ for its simplicity.

12. February 21, 1828, is a special day in the history of the Cherokee people. After that date, thanks to Sequoya, they no longer _____ a newspaper in their own language.

13. The Cherokees could read in their own newspapers what was happening to them as a people. This was one of the many _____ they enjoyed from having a written language.

14. Sequoya kept busy all his life. In his later years he chose to travel and study other Native American languages rather than leading a life of _____.

15. The heads of the National Park Service found a way to honor Sequoya. They _____ that Sequoia National Park in California be named after him.

Name: _____   Date: _____

Lesson 2

1. Sequoias are found only in certain parts of California. Temperature and the dryness of the air both _____ growing conditions.

2. The best way to get to Sequoia National Park is by car. You don't need a _____ to visit there.

3. Unlike redwoods, sequoias do not grow well along the California coast. They prefer the colder, dryer _____ found inland.

4. Forest fires do little harm to fully grown redwoods and sequoias. A fire may _____ the trees' outside bark but seldom lasts long enough to burn right through.

5. The bark of these forest giants needs to be thick to save them from forest fires. On a fully grown tree, the bark can _____ twelve inches in thickness.

6. California's redwood trees remind some people of a Greek temple. Their great trunks do look like huge marble _____.

7. A single redwood tree would be hard to miss. It would _____ over everything around it.

8. It is unusual to see a single redwood tree. Redwood trees usually grow in _____.

9. Redwood trees can live for several thousand years. To do so, they have to be able to _____ diseases that kill other trees.

10. It's not easy to climb a tall redwood tree. There may be no _____ to hold onto for a hundred feet or more above the ground.

11. Giant redwoods are among the largest living things on the planet. These _____ trees can grow to almost 400 feet in height.

12. It's possible to find out how much wood a redwood's trunk contains. You can _____ the amount if you know the height of the tree and its thickness at the top and bottom.

13. It is safe to leave outdoor furniture in the rain if the furniture is made from redwood. Unlike other kinds of wood, redwood is slow to _____.

14. Cutting down redwood trees for lumber is allowed in some parts of California. However, it is _____ in Redwood National Park.

15. It is easy to see the difference between full-grown redwoods and younger ones. Trees that are _____ are taller and have thicker trunks.

Lesson 3

1. Many animals cannot live in cold weather. Some move to where it is warmer, while others deal with winter by _____.

2. Woodchucks can stay in the same area year round. Unlike many other animals, they don't need to _____ to a warmer place to get through the winter.

3. Moles and woodchucks are alike in some ways. Both animals live in _____ that they dig.

4. Woodchucks gather leaves and grass in the fall to make underground nests. They _____ inside their nests to keep warm over the winter.

5. In a _____ winter, a woodchuck can freeze to death if it does not dig a deep-enough nest.

6. A woodchuck first builds its nest and then closes off the tunnel leading to it. When it has finished these _____, it is ready to begin its long winter sleep.

7. During the winter months, woodchucks do not eat. With the _____ of spring, they start getting hungry.

8. Woodchucks are not active in the winter months. Going into a deep sleep greatly _____ the amount of oxygen they need.

9. A woodchuck in a deep sleep does not seem to be alive. If you checked its heart, you might think it had _____ beating altogether.

10. You are unlikely to see woodchucks in January. They do not _____ from their nests in the middle of winter.

11. Food is the first thing that woodchucks look for after they wake up. They are _____ after not eating for several months.

12. Woodchucks and rabbits can both do a lot of damage in a garden. Woodchucks are more _____ than rabbits because they eat more.

13. The weather on February 2nd is supposed to affect the length of winter. If it's sunny, Punxsutawney Phil can _____ his shadow, and spring is still six weeks away.

14. Punxsutawney Phil is not very active when he first pokes his head above ground. He probably still feels _____ after his long sleep.

15. The story of Punxsutawney Phil is just a legend. Woodchucks can't really _____ how much longer winter will last.

Lesson 4

1. Sucheng's parents were unable to send her to school until she was eight. Their _____ income did not permit spending on her education.

2. Polio was once greatly feared. People _____ to the disease became ill and often lost the use of their limbs.

3. Her illness greatly affected Sucheng's life. Once she had been a very _____ child, but now she was forced to spend all her time in bed.

4. Sucheng's world became smaller when her illness forced her to stay in bed. She felt that her world had _____ to the size of her bedroom.

5. Sucheng supported herself by holding onto the backs of chairs. _____ bars like those used in gymnastics would have made it easier for her to practice walking.

6. The brave little girl fell many times while supporting herself against the chairs. She was so _____ to walk again that she put up with the pain.

7. Sucheng's parents could not have imagined her later success. They would have been _____ to know that she would become a history professor in the United States.

8. An important year in China's history was 1948. That was when communist rule was _____ on the country.

9. Sucheng's parents did not welcome the communist takeover of China. They were _____ about what this would mean for the country.

10. Because they _____ freedom too much to want to live under communist rule, Sucheng's parents thought often about leaving China.

11. Sucheng's parents were dismayed when the situation in China became worse. Their _____ was to leave the country and settle in Malaysia.

12. Her piano teacher must have been impressed by Sucheng's playing. The young girl was asked to give piano _____ at the school.

13. As soon as she began to play, Sucheng's _____ hands flew over the piano keys.

14. Sucheng went to high school in Malaysia. Later, after moving to the United States, she _____ the University of Hawaii.

15. After her recovery, doctors warned Sucheng that she might need a wheelchair some day. They feared that her _____ from polio could return when she got older.

Lesson 5

1. The life of Hans Christian Andersen is a very interesting one. "A Life That Changed" offers only a brief _____ into the writer's life.

2. As a little boy, Hans liked to write his own plays. Afterward, he would stage them in the little _____ theater his father made for him.

3. Hans was eleven when his father died. The three-year period that followed, until he left for Copenhagen, was the unhappiest _____ of the young boy's life.

4. Hans, with his odd ways and habit of staring off into space, was not like his fellow workers. They must have thought of his behavior as very _____.

5. If Hans had overheard the remarks of his fellow workers, he would have known they felt _____ for him

6. The cruel jokes played on Hans by his fellow workers must have upset him greatly. He had always been a very _____ child, protected by his parents.

7. Hans must have been nervous about asking his mother if he could leave home. He must have been afraid that she would _____ the idea.

8. Hans was so eager to leave home that he _____ until his mother agreed to let him go to Copenhagen.

9. Andersen did not start out writing children's stories. He _____ many different kinds of writing first.

10. Andersen showed his plays to theater owners in Copenhagen. Sadly, he could not _____ them to put on his plays.

11. Anderson was a complete failure as a writer of plays. He did not _____ success until he began writing children's stories.

12. When writing a play, Andersen must have thought back to his childhood. He would have _____ the plays he put on in his little toy theater.

13. "The Ugly Ducking" tells the story of a duckling that turned out to be a swan. In the story, the change from an ugly duckling to a beautiful swan is gradual rather than _____.

14. Some of the people who turned down his plays must have heard of Andersen after he became famous. They would have had to _____ their opinion of him.

15. The world owes a great debt to Hans Christian Andersen. His stories have _____ millions of children for more than one hundred and fifty years.

Lesson 6

1. Only the best was good enough for the emperor. Naturally. he wanted to wear only the most _____ clothes.

2. The emperor believed the story the two tailors told him. Any attempts by the ministers to tell him the truth would probably have been in _____.

3. The emperor didn't care how much the new clothes cost. He _____ to pay the two tailors whatever they asked.

4. The tailors told the ministers that the work was going very well. The _____ that they reported was actually a lie.

5. The ministers pretended they could see the emperor's new clothes. This proved that they had _____ taste.

6. The tailors were taking a big risk. Their _____ plan would work only if they could fool the emperor and the ministers.

7. The emperor thought that he was beautifully dressed. Actually, his _____ wardrobe was made up only of his underwear.

8. The emperor's new clothes were invisible. No matter how long you _____, you'd never be able to see them.

9. The emperor believed he looked magnificent as he walked the streets of the town. He never again wanted to be wearing his _____ old clothes.

10. The emperor believed that all the people loved him. He liked nothing better than hearing the _____ of the crowd.

11. A small voice was heard coming from the crowd. It was a little boy _____ that the emperor had no clothes.

12. The emperor enjoyed hearing the cheers of the townspeople. It was not until he heard some of them laughing at him that he became _____.

13. The emperor was used to hearing only what those around him wanted him to hear. The _____ of the crowd must have been a great shock to him.

14. The little boy spoiled the emperor's fun. He _____ the truth, which his ministers had been afraid to tell him.

15. The emperor must have been eager to find the two tailors when he returned to the palace. The _____ were probably not eager to be found.

Lesson 7

1. There are many kinds of octopuses in the world. A map of the many oceans where they are found shows how widely they are _____.

2. Octopuses hardly ever venture into deep water. They prefer to stay in _____ water, not far from shore.

3. An octopus has no skeleton. This makes it possible for the octopus to squeeze its _____ body into all kinds of narrow spaces.

4. One of the ways an octopus protects itself is by changing color. It can do this in an _____.

5. The octopus is able to _____ its color to make itself harder to be seen.

6. The octopus can change quickly from brown to green to gray. It does this to match the color of its _____.

7. Sharks and other large fish hunt octopuses. However, the octopus has an extremely _____ sense of danger and will often escape.

8. A shark closing in on an octopus may not get the meal it seeks. The octopus has several different ways to _____ the attacker.

9. The octopus has several good ways of defending itself against an attack. One way is to _____ a black liquid that makes the water cloudy and the octopus difficult to see.

10. Crabs and other small creatures on the ocean floor are in danger if an octopus is near. If a crab sees an octopus coming after it, the crab will _____ away to try to hide.

11. The octopus can easily get at the meat in a lobster. It is _____ with a strong, horny beak that it uses to crack open the shell.

12. Movies sometimes misrepresent the octopus as a terrifying monster by showing a human being as the _____ of one of these usually gentle sea creatures.

13. An octopus will sometimes wrap its arms around a swimmer. The best way to escape the octopus's _____ is to stop struggling.

14. Octopuses try to stay away from people in the water. Even a very large Pacific octopus is unlikely to try to _____ someone swimming nearby.

15. Should a large octopus wrap its arms around you, don't struggle. An octopus is more likely to let you go if you let your body go _____.

Name: _____   Date: _____

Lesson 8

1. Antipater wrote of the Seven Wonders more than two thousand years ago. The Great Pyramid was _____ even at that time.

2. People can climb up the sides of the Great Pyramid today. That was impossible when it was first built because the _____ then was perfectly smooth.

3. It takes a long time to make the difficult climb up the side of the Great Pyramid. And it takes just as long to _____.

4. The Great Pyramid seems like solid stone, but it contains a large number of rooms. Many of these _____ are quite large.

5. The Great Pyramid was built especially for King Cheops. Of course, the most _____ and splendid of the rooms was set aside for him.

6. It was possible to move about inside the Great Pyramid. A number of _____ ran from room to room.

7. The pyramid builders did not have to bring stone for the Great Pyramid from far away. A nearby _____ had all the material needed.

8. To reach higher levels, the pyramid builders piled up earth against the side of the pyramid. The _____ got higher and longer as the work progressed.

9. Daylight did not reach inside the pyramid. Workers would have needed lighted torches to find their way through its dark _____.

10. King Cheops was buried with _____ objects he had used while alive, including gold plates and fine jewels.

11. The dead king's needs were taken care of inside the pyramid. _____ of food were left out for him in case he grew hungry.

12. After the dead king was placed in the chamber, the pyramid builders carefully sealed off his resting place. They did not want him to become a victim of _____.

13. The people who had prepared the king's resting place took a last look around. They then closed off the _____ with big granite slabs.

14. It is astounding that the Great Pyramid has lasted for so long. It has stood there in the sands of Egypt for forty-five _____.

15. You can easily find Cairo on a map of the Middle East. This large city near the Great Pyramid is _____ in Egypt, which is a country in North Africa.

Lesson 9

1. Over three-quarters of a million people live in San Francisco today. It's hard to believe it was once a _____ of just two thousand people.

2. The choice in 1849 was to stay home and work for a dollar a day or go west and hope to get rich. Whatever the decision, many forty-niners were _____ by fears that they had made the wrong choice.

3. Those who joined the gold rush had many worries. Their greatest _____ was that they might never make it back home.

4. The two ways to get to California were by ship or by covered wagon. The _____ of traveling by covered wagon was that families could go together and take more goods with them.

5. Cattle and horses suffered crossing the desert. There was little water and the land was too _____ for grass to grow.

6. The journey by ship from New York to San Francisco took six months. The _____ between the two places by sea was seventeen thousand miles.

7. Not every ship made it safely around the tip of South America. Many struck rocks and _____, drowning everyone aboard.

8. Some of the forty-niners went west to work at regular jobs. However, most traveled to California for the _____ purpose of finding gold.

9. The families who stayed behind waited eagerly for letters from their loved ones in California. News of what was happening out there was _____, so all they could do was hope.

10. Sam Brannan had something important to tell anyone who would listen. Those who heard him were _____ to learn that gold had been discovered at Sutter's Mill.

11. People were willing to pay Brannan fifteen dollars for a twenty-cent dish. This _____ the truth of the saying that something is worth what someone else will pay for it.

12. Sam Brannan became so rich that he could print his own money. Obviously, he was not a _____ Californian.

13. It was not just Americans who headed for California. The San Francisco waterfront was flooded with _____ of people arriving by ship from all over the world.

14. By 1850, most of the "easy" gold had been discovered. The _____ of newcomers finding gold after that time were very slim.

15. Gold miners could make lots of money during the gold rush. Those who were _____ used their money to buy land in and around San Francisco.

Lesson 10

1. In the Japanese folktale, Tokoyo worked as a pearl diver searching for oysters on the seabed. The story does not say how her father earned his _____.

2. Tokoyo's mother died when she was just a baby. Losing her father was the second great _____ to affect the young girl.

3. When her father was taken away, Tokoyo felt parentless. She wasn't an actual _____, of course, because her father was still alive.

4. Even though the emperor was powerful, he didn't get everything he wanted. What he _____ most was an end to all his illnesses.

5. The emperor had many things wrong with him. There were plenty of _____ for his doctors to observe.

6. Tokoyo was not allowed to write to her father. If she had tried to _____ with him, the emperor's soldiers would probably have taken her away, too.

7. Her friends had no need to ask why Tokoyo was sad. They knew that what _____ the young girl was the loss of her father.

8. Tokoyo was not allowed to visit or write to her father. She was unable to _____ him on the distant island.

9. Tokoyo didn't need to ask the girl who was ready to dive from the top of the cliff if she was afraid. She could tell the girl was terrified because she was _____ in fear.

10. The evil sea god and Tokoyo came face to face. The battle took place in the ocean's _____ and ended with the monster's death.

11. Those on top of the cliff saw Tokoyo swimming safely back to the shore. They knew then that she had _____ the evil sea god.

12. After diving from the _____, Tokoyo swam back to shore and rejoined the others.

13. The death of the evil sea god didn't happen by accident. Tokoyo intended to kill the monster, and her action was quite _____.

14. Tokoyo's father would always be in her debt. Were it not for his brave daughter, he would never have _____ his freedom.

15. Everyone likes a story with a happy ending. Sadness is _____ at the end of the story when Tokoyo and her father are happily reunited.

Name: _____   Date: _____

Lesson 11

1. Some people are not satisfied with a single visit to New England. They enjoy making _____ trips to that part of the country just to admire the fall colors of the maple trees.

2. People plan months ahead for a visit to Vermont, Maine, or New Hampshire. They have a _____ of how beautiful a fall day in New England can be.

3. In the early fall, the maple trees are ablaze with color. By late fall the _____ is gone and the trees are bare.

4. We can get from two to four pounds of syrup from a single maple tree. A hundred trees will probably _____ close to three hundred pounds of syrup.

5. It's difficult to tell ahead of time how much sap a particular tree will produce. The amount _____ from year to year.

6. Maple trees in upper, dryer areas produce smaller amounts of sap. This sap requires less boiling, however, because of the _____ amount of sugar it contains.

7. A bucket is hung on a peg below the hole. The hole has been _____ in the trunk, fairly close to the ground.

8. Native Americans were not equipped with drills. Instead of making holes in the trunks of the maple trees, they made _____ in them.

9. Up to twenty gallons of sap can be collected from a healthy sugar maple. This amount is _____ and produces up to four pounds of syrup.

10. You might think the tree needs the sap more than people need syrup. Fortunately, there is enough sap produced to _____ both the tree and maple syrup lovers.

11. Syrup makers boil the sap in large kettles. Great clouds of steam rise from the kettles as the water _____.

12. Refined maple syrup is clear and a light golden brown. _____ maple syrup is darker.

13. Makers of pancake syrup prepare the flavorings carefully. They want to make the _____ kind of syrup taste as much like the real thing as possible.

14. Some pancake syrup is made mostly from corn. The _____ may contain only a small amount of real maple syrup.

15. Corn syrup by itself is almost colorless. Maple syrup, however, usually has a golden-brown _____.

Lesson 12

1. Koko is very different from gorillas in the wild. For one thing, the gorillas living in the African rain forest are much less _____.

2. While she was still a baby, Koko became very ill. She _____ under the care of Dr. Patterson.

3. Koko soon learned to communicate using American Sign Language (ASL). If she wanted something, she had to make the _____ by signing.

4. Those who have difficulty hearing can choose from several systems. ASL is the _____ method of communication for many of them.

5. Dr. Patterson won Koko's trust by staying close to her. The two were hardly ever _____ from each other.

6. Koko has many different moods. She can be sad or happy, and she can get _____ when something annoys her.

7. Koko made it very plain that stuffed animals did not make her happy. Holding a real kitten was _____ for Koko.

8. After Koko threw away the stuffed animal, Dr. Patterson knew what to do. A real kitten soon _____ the toy kitten.

9. Koko soon discovered that the second kitten was real. She did not have to be _____ to play with the real kitten.

10. Gorilla and kitten were able to communicate. All Ball liked Koko's _____ of stroking her fur.

11. Koko took All Ball for rides. The kitten _____ tightly to the fur on the gorilla's back.

12. Koko liked to stroke All Ball. All Ball enjoyed being _____ because Koko was so gentle.

13. When Koko was happy, she liked being with people. When she was unhappy, she _____ even Dr. Patterson's company.

14. People who say animals don't have feelings should have seen Koko when All Ball died. They would have seen the gorilla _____ for days.

15. Dr. Patterson proved that gorillas have the _____ to communicate with humans.

Lesson 13

1. The German army marched first into France and Belgium. The _____ of Holland followed soon after.

2. Holland tried to resist when Germany moved against it. Its army was _____ by the much more powerful German army.

3. Once the Dutch defenses were broken, the German army marched into Holland. Within a very short time they had _____ the entire country.

4. People found it hard to believe Hitler's intentions could be so evil. The _____ truth is that he planned to murder every Jewish person in Europe.

5. Hitler was a _____, an evil person with extreme beliefs and a very strong will.

6. Eight people lived in the cramped space behind a bookshelf in Mr. Frank's office. They were completely _____ from the outside world.

7. For two years outsiders were free to enter Mr. Frank's office. No one _____ that people were hiding behind the bookshelf.

8. The Frank family and their friends had to be extremely quiet. They were _____ that if they made noise they would be discovered.

9. The group hiding in the cramped space had to rely on each other. They tried to cheer each other up when they started to feel _____.

10. Writing in her diary was important to Anne. The activity was an escape from the _____ life she was forced to lead.

11. Anne had something to hope for while in hiding. She was _____ on Britain and America to free all of them from Nazi rule.

12. A friend of Anne's family secretly kept Anne's diary. The fact that she had kept a diary was not _____ until after the war.

13. Anne Frank's diary has sold millions of copies. It had an enormous _____ on the world when it was first published.

14. The Nazis boasted that their rule over Europe would last for a thousand years. Although their power was much more _____, lasting only from 1932 to 1945, the Nazis murdered millions of people during these years.

15. The Nazi party promised to make Germany great again. Their rule was an enormous _____ not just for Germany but also for the whole world.

Lesson 14

1. There was nothing fancy about the cottage where Huw and his mother lived. It really wasn't much to _____ about.

2. You could paint a picture of the scene where the cows gather around Huw. There's the blue of the sky, the green of the _____, and the six silver cows.

3. The silver cows were drawn to Huw's music. We don't know whether it was just the sound of the harp or the particular _____ he played.

4. The silver cows gathered around Huw as he played. The music from his harp _____ them much pleasure.

5. The cows Huw brought home that first night were not ordinary cows. You'd expect to get _____ milk from such unusual cows.

6. Huw's mother refused to change her mind about calling the butcher. Had she _____, the story might have had a different ending.

7. Huw argued with his mother as long as he dared. He was forced to _____ himself before her by obeying her order to be quiet.

8. Huw did not agree with his mother. In the end he had to _____ to her will since she was the parent and he was the child.

9. Huw and his mother both had strong wills and neither liked to give in to the other. It seems they could both be _____.

10. The butcher agreed to come the next day. It was _____ for the cow that the butcher didn't come right away.

11. You could tell how unhappy Huw was by the way he walked. His feet seemed too heavy to lift as he _____ up the mountain.

12. Huw's mother made a lot of money from the milk the silver cows gave. Her income must have _____ when the cows returned to the lake.

13. If Huw hadn't thrown away the harp, the cows might not have returned to the lake. If some-one had asked if he had been responsible for the loss of the cows, Huw would have had to _____ guilty.

14. There were no water lilies growing in the middle of the lake. They grew only along the _____.

15. At the end of the story, Huw and his mother both feel sad at the loss of the silver cows. The story ends on a rather _____ note.

Lesson 15

1. For several centuries, the bald eagle was fair game for hunters. There was little _____ for the fate of this magnificent bird.

2. People used to shoot bald eagles in order to have them stuffed. Today, people shoot them with cameras and have photographs as _____.

3. The bald eagle has exquisite hunting skills. A small animal on the ground may not even see the great bird before it _____ and carries away its victim.

4. Even small lambs and piglets are not safe from the bald eagle's claws. Its _____ are big enough to clutch small animals and carry them off.

5. In the 1950s, it was found that bald eagles' shells were very thin. Of course, the thinner they are the more _____ they are.

6. DDT came into use in the 1950s. Too much attention had been given to the benefits of this pesticide, but the risks had not been properly _____.

7. The pesticide was thought to be safe when it was first used. Later it was shown to be a serious _____ to fish and to the birds that survive by eating them.

8. Rachel Carson wrote a book with an important message for the world. Her book _____ on one thing: the destructive use of pesticides.

9. Carson's book, *Silent Spring*, became an instant best seller. Its _____ sales helped make its author famous.

10. Until *Silent Spring* was published, the problem of DDT had been ignored. Rachel Carson's book _____ demands for the United States Congress to act.

11. Carson's book changed the way Americans thought about pesticides. It became _____ that Congress would have to forbid the use of certain pesticides.

12. In 1973, Congress passed a law to save endangered birds and animals. As a result of this action, shooting bald eagles was _____ in the United States

13. By the 1950s, the bald eagle had almost died out in the lower forty-eight states. Figures from 2001, in _____, showed over five thousand breeding pairs.

14. Bird watchers who counted bald eagles in the 1950s were very pessimistic about the bird's future. The more _____ past gives them reason to be more hopeful.

15. We can take pride in the fact that the number of bald eagles is on the rise. It would have been tragic if this _____ of America had disappeared from our skies forever.

Lesson 16

1. In his youth he was known as John Chapman. Most people know him by the more _____ name of Johnny Appleseed.

2. At first only a few people had heard of Johnny Appleseed. Then the story of what he had done _____, and today almost everyone knows his name.

3. Chapman took life moment by moment. He didn't think about where he would spend the night until _____ was approaching.

4. Sleeping indoors or outdoors made no difference to Johnny Appleseed. It was his _____ to sleep in the open when he couldn't find shelter for the night.

5. No one could say that Johnny Appleseed was a vain person. His _____ clothes showed that the opposite was true.

6. Johnny Appleseed's needs were few and his wants even fewer. By not owning things that would have tied him down, he found _____.

7. Chapman would rather shiver in the dark than hurt a living creature. Once he _____ his fire because mosquitoes were drawn to the flames.

8. Chapman did not have to use his walking stick as a weapon. If he had needed to, the stick was _____ enough to keep an animal from attacking him.

9. Johnny Appleseed was the kindest and gentlest of men. He was loved by everyone who knew him and was _____ by no one.

10. When he left an area, Johnny Appleseed's friends knew he'd be back. He was _____ to revisit places he'd been to earlier.

11. As to where he would be next month, Johnny Appleseed had no idea. He followed no particular plan but_____ wherever his fancy led him.

12. Johnny Appleseed had no interest in making money from the trees that he planted. The _____ he started were his gift to the local people.

13. Spring and fall were special times of the year. In spring the _____ were filled with pink and white flowers, and in the fall they were thick with juicy apples.

14. Johnny Appleseed found things to do even in the winter months. That was the best time of year to _____ the trees he'd planted.

15. The people of the Ohio River Valley had reason to be grateful to John Chapman. Until he came along, it was almost impossible to _____ apples there.

Name: _____ Date: _____

Lesson 17

1. This is not a tale of great adventures or bravery in battle. There are no _____ deeds in this simple story of African village life.

2. Even though he was rich, the *tajiri* was too mean to give anything away. He was so _____ he hated to part with the smells from his kitchen.

3. The *tajiri* ate the finest foods that his cooks could prepare. The *maskini* lived on much more modest _____.

4. The *maskini* made himself comfortable outside the rich man's kitchen. He was waiting for the smell of the food to come _____ through the window.

5. We know that the *tajiri* was rich and the *maskini* poor, but we don't know their ages. The story doesn't tell us which was the _____ of the two.

6. The *maskini* had not expected to spend the night in jail. He was _____ there by the *tajiri*'s servants.

7. The *maskini* may not have wanted to go to the court, but he had no choice. A person who was _____ had to show up in court.

8. The *tajiri* looked sure of himself because he believed there was no doubt he would win. The *maskini* looked _____ because he expected to lose.

9. The *tajiri* demanded that he be given the *maskini*'s goat. He would have _____ the poor man of the only thing he owned.

10. The *maskini* must have been a rather shy person. Even though he was given the chance, he chose not to _____ the court.

11. Actually, there was no need for the *maskini* to say anything. The court decided that the *tajiri*'s argument lacked _____.

12. The *maskini* humbled the rich man in court. There would be no _____ welcome for him if he later tried to visit the *tajiri*.

13. The court decided correctly. The rich man was allowed to _____ the smell from the *maskini*'s goat whenever he wanted.

14. Everyone can agree that the *tajiri* deserved to lose the case. No one would _____ of his taking the *maskini* to court.

15. Everyone likes a happy ending. At the _____ of this story, the court decides correctly, even though the *tajiri* might not agree.

Wordly Wise 3000 Book

Lesson 18

1. Shi Huang-ti stopped the fighting that went on among the Chinese warlords. These _____ had caused much suffering among the people.

2. The emperor was not concerned about someone wishing him harm from within China. He worried about _____ enemies.

3. Shi Huang-ti had to worry about where an invading force might come from. The danger from the north was no _____ matter, and the emperor took it seriously.

4. The emperor would build the wall where the need was greatest. He decided the _____ to China was from the north.

5. Building an enormous wall that would run for fifteen hundred miles was not easy. This _____ effort was made possible by the work of many thousands of Chinese workers.

6. The wheelbarrow had not been invented when the Great Wall was built. Humans were _____ to do the carrying.

7. Men and women from China's farms built the Great Wall. These _____ had no choice when the emperor's men called upon them to work.

8. The wall is thicker at the bottom than at the top. Its _____ at the top almost equals the wall's twenty-five foot height.

9. Every few miles along the Great Wall were _____. These structures housed soldiers whose job it was to protect a section of the wall.

10. Soldiers could march ten _____ along the top of the wall. This made it possible for a number of soldiers to move fairly quickly.

11. The Great Wall was built to make invasions from the north more difficult. It probably did reduce the _____ of attacks from the northern tribes.

12. Just looking at the Great Wall might have scared off enemy tribes. A wall twenty-five feet high manned by armed soldiers is a difficult _____ to cross.

13. The Great Wall was built as far north as Chinese people would go. It was not safe to venture beyond China's northern _____.

14. Shi Huang-ti built many fine buildings, including a magnificent palace. It was located in the empire's _____.

15. The Great Wall was Shi Huang-ti's greatest achievement. It _____ that his name would be remembered thousands of years after his death.

Name: _____   Date: _____

Lesson 19

1. In the 1920s, hardly anyone had heard of modern dance. The _____ style of dancing at that time was classical ballet.

2. Martha Graham had no use for exquisite costumes and artificial settings. By _____ what wasn't needed, she greatly simplified dance.

3. Ruth St. Denis and Ted Shawn gave Graham a chance to perform. They _____ her talent and put her under contract.

4. Martha Graham swept aside all the old ways of thinking about dance. She started a new _____ that was different in every way.

5. With each fresh venture, Graham broke new ground. At the same time, she _____ the taste of the American public.

6. She _____ only female dancers for many years because she wanted American women to be able to have greater freedom.

7. Graham drew on American poetry and history as she thought about new dances. The greatest _____ of ideas was her own imagination.

8. Graham first _____ and hired male dancers in 1938.

9. Graham saw what she had to do and went ahead and did it. Her tough attitude to life is reflected in her dances, which are never _____.

10. She picked her two best students and invited them to join her in performing in public as a _____.

11. New York was not the only city in which people could enjoy her recitals. By taking her company on _____, Graham showed the rest of the country what modern dance was.

12. Very few people were disappointed by a Martha Graham recital. She _____ just about everyone who saw her perform.

13. Graham decided that she could not devote enough time to both teaching and performing. She had to _____ one or the other.

14. Graham achieved a great deal during her life. Many people feel that the Martha Graham Dance Company was her greatest _____.

15. Graham was working on a dance piece when she died at the age of ninety-six. She felt it was _____ to keep working right to the end.

Lesson 20

1. Seven hundred years ago, Switzerland fell under Austrian occupation. An Austrian named Gessler was at the _____ of the Swiss government, and he hated the Swiss people.

2. The Swiss had every reason to detest the Austrian governor. He was _____ of every kind of cruelty, and they were his victims.

3. The Swiss were a proud people, but they felt helpless. They were _____ that their country was ruled by a foreign power.

4. There was no love lost between Gessler and the Swiss people. He _____ them and they felt the same way about him.

5. Gessler could make the townspeople bow their heads, but he couldn't make them smile. Their _____ faces revealed their true feelings.

6. William Tell's son knew that he had to stay perfectly still. He didn't move when he father shot the arrow, but perhaps his lip _____ slightly.

7. If the first arrow had hurt his son, William Tell was ready. It would take only an instant to _____ the second arrow in the groove of his crossbow and shoot Gessler.

8. After learning what the second arrow was for, Gessler was sorry that he had been so amiable. He had been too quick to _____ his prisoner.

9. Gessler could feel the contempt in William Tell's voice. He felt that Tell had _____ him in front of many people

10. Gessler ordered William Tell to be locked up for the rest of his life. He had no intention of ever _____ his prisoner.

11. William Tell accepted his punishment without saying a word. He was too proud to _____ Gessler to show mercy.

12. Those on board cowered below in fear. It seemed that only the rocks ahead could _____ the movement of the boat.

13. The crew knew what would happen if they struck the rocks. The sides of the boat would be _____, and it would quickly sink, drowning them.

14. The story does not tell what happened to the rest of the people on the boat. We do not know whether they were_____ saved.

15. Ask in the town of Altdorf whether William Tell was a real person. Few people will _____ that their statue is that of someone who once lived.

Lesson Review Answer Key

Lesson 1

1. sufficient
2. patriotism
3. uttered
4. complete
5. master
6. developed
7. dismayed
8. project
9. represent
10. hailed
11. remarkable
l2. lacked
13. benefits
14. ease
15. recommended

Lesson 2

1. affect
2. permit
3. climate
4. scorch
5. exceed
6. columns
7. tower
8. groves
9. resist
10. limbs
11. mammoth
12. calculate
13. decay
14. forbidden
15. mature

Lesson 3

1. hibernating
2. migrate
3. burrows
4. nestle
5. severe
6. preparations
7. approach
8. reduces
9. ceased
10. venture
11. famished
12. destructive
13. observe
14. drowsy
15. forecast

Lesson 4

1. modest
2. exposed
3. active
4. contracted
5. Parallel
6. eager
7. astounded
8. imposed
9. pessimistic
10. cherished
11. response
12. recitals
13. graceful
14. attended
15. paralysis

Lesson 5

1. glimpse
2. mock
3. phase
4. quaint
5. contempt
6. sensitive
7. reject
8. persisted
9. attempted
10. persuade
11. achieve
12. recalled
13. abrupt
14. revise
15. entertained

Lesson 6

1. exquisite
2. vain
3. intended
4. progress
5. refined
6. crafty
7. entire
8. peered
9. drab
10. applause
11. exclaiming
12. uneasy
13. jeers
14. disclosed
15. scoundrels

Lesson 7

1. distributed
2. shallow
3. flexible
4. instant
5. alter
6. surroundings
7. keen
8. confuse
9. eject
10. scurry
11. equipped
12. victim
13. embrace
14. seize
15. limp

Lesson 8

1. ancient
2. surface
3. descend
4. chambers
5. spacious
6. passages
7. quarry
8. ramp
9. interior
10. precious
11. Portions
12. intruders
13. entry
14. centuries
15. located

Lesson 9

1. hamlet
2. tormented
3. misgiving
4. advantage
5. parched
6. distance
7. foundered
8. sole
9. scarce
10. astonished
11. confirms
12. typical
13. hosts
14. prospects
15. shrewd

Lesson 10

1. livelihood
2. misfortune
3. orphan
4. desired
5. symptoms
6. communicate
7. ailed
8. console
9. cowering
10. depths
11. slain
12. precipice
13. deliberate
14. regained
15. banished

Lesson 11

1. annual
2. vision
3. foliage
4. yield
5. varies
6. increased
7. bored
8. gashes
9. considerable
10. nourish
11. evaporates
12. Crude
13. artificial
14. blend
15. hue

Lesson 12

1. amiable
2. recovered
3. request
4. preferred
5. separated
6. furious
7. bliss
8. replaced
9. coaxed
10. gesture
11. clutched
12. caressed
13. shunned
14. mope
15. ability

Lesson 13

1. invasion
2. routed
3. occupied
4. appalling
5. fanatic
6. isolated
7. suspected
8. terrified
9. dejected
10. dreary
11. depending
12. revealed
13. impact
14. temporary
15. tragedy

Lesson 14

1. boast
2. meadow
3. chords
4. afforded
5. exceptional
6. relented
7. humble
8. submit
9. obstinate
10. fortunate
11. trudged
12. plunged
13. plead
14. fringes
15. melancholy

Lesson 15

1. concern
2. trophies
3. pounces
4. talons
5. fragile
6. considered
7. menace
8. concentrated
9. widespread
10. prompted
11. apparent
12. banned
13. contrast
14. recent
15. symbol

Lesson 16

1. familiar
2. blossomed
3. dusk
4. practice
5. threadbare
6. contentment
7. extinguished
8. stout
9. detested
10. apt
11. wandered
12. orchards
13. boughs
14. prune
15. obtain

Lesson 17

1. valiant
2. stingy
3. fare
4. wafting
5. elder
6. escorted
7. summoned
8. forlorn
9. deprived
10. address
11. merit
12. hearty
13. inhale
14. approve
15. conclusion

Lesson 18

1. feuds
2. external
3. petty
4. threat
5. vast
6. utilized
7. peasants
8. breadth
9. fortresses
10. abreast
11. frequency
12. barrier
13. frontier
14. capital
15. ensured

Lesson 19

1. foremost
2. eliminating
3. recognized
4. tradition
5. elevated
6. engaged
7. source
8. auditioned
9. sentimental
10. trio
11. tour
12. entranced
13. forsake
14. creation
15. essential

Lesson 20

1. helm
2. capable
3. outraged
4. despised
5. sullen
6. quivered
7. insert
8. congratulate
9. humiliated
10. releasing
11. implore
12. arrest
13. pierced
14. eventually
15. dispute

Book 4 Tests

Book 4, Lesson 1 Test

Choose the BEST way to complete each sentence or answer each question. Then fill in the circle next to your answer.

1. <u>Hail</u> is

   Ⓐ   light snow.

   Ⓑ   frozen rain.

   Ⓒ   heavy rain.

   Ⓓ   light rain.

2. When you <u>complete</u> a job, you

   Ⓐ   finish it.

   Ⓑ   agree to do it.

   Ⓒ   do it well.

   Ⓓ   fail to do it.

3. Which is a <u>sufficient</u> amount of food?

   Ⓐ   too much food

   Ⓑ   almost enough food

   Ⓒ   enough food

   Ⓓ   food that is left over

4. A <u>patriot</u> is someone who

   Ⓐ   lives in a certain country.

   Ⓑ   was born in a certain country.

   Ⓒ   loves his or her country.

   Ⓓ   leaves his or her country.

5. When you <u>hail</u> someone, you

   Ⓐ   laugh at him or her.

   Ⓑ   vote for him or her.

   Ⓒ   greet him or her.

   Ⓓ   send him or her a package.

6. A <u>remark</u> is a

    Ⓐ   loud bang.

    Ⓑ   shout.

    Ⓒ   whisper.

    Ⓓ   comment.

7. To <u>master</u> an art is to

    Ⓐ   teach others how to do it.

    Ⓑ   become skilled at it.

    Ⓒ   struggle to learn it.

    Ⓓ   admire artists' work.

8. To <u>represent</u> others is to

    Ⓐ   act in their place.

    Ⓑ   fight them.

    Ⓒ   follow them.

    Ⓓ   join with them.

9. If you are at <u>ease</u>, how do you feel?

    Ⓐ   bored

    Ⓑ   alert

    Ⓒ   sleepy

    Ⓓ   comfortable

10. If you are <u>dismayed</u>, you would probably feel

    Ⓐ   curious.

    Ⓑ   comfortable.

    Ⓒ   very worried.

    Ⓓ   hungry.

11. To <u>project</u> a movie is to

    Ⓐ   show it on a screen.

    Ⓑ   plan to see it.

    Ⓒ   tell others about it.

    Ⓓ   find it in a video rental store.

12. Ms. Pine <u>recommends</u> Mario's Restaurant. This means that she

&Ⓐ works there.

Ⓑ owns the restaurant.

Ⓒ has never been to Mario's.

Ⓓ says Mario's is a good place to eat.

13. Why would a school have a <u>benefit</u>?

Ⓐ to raise money for the school

Ⓑ to give parents and teachers a chance to meet one another

Ⓒ to test students' reading and math skills

Ⓓ to hire new teachers for the school

14. Carmina has a new <u>project</u>. She has

Ⓐ a brand-new outfit.

Ⓑ a fancy new bicycle.

Ⓒ a new plan for organizing her baseball cards.

Ⓓ made friends with students at her new school.

15. My dog has <u>remarkable</u> intelligence. He is

Ⓐ about as smart as most dogs.

Ⓑ unusually smart.

Ⓒ not very smart.

Ⓓ unusually stupid.

16. If someone says, "Please don't <u>utter</u> a word," what should you do?

Ⓐ do not write anything down

Ⓑ do not hesitate to say what you think

Ⓒ do not say anything at all

Ⓓ do not send any e-mail messages

17. Dr. Boynton <u>recommends</u> plenty of exercise. This means that she

Ⓐ doesn't like exercise.

Ⓑ exercises regularly.

Ⓒ suggests that her patients exercise regularly.

Ⓓ cautions her patients not to exercise too hard.

18. "Shelby looks very healthy," Dr. Boynton <u>remarked</u>. In this sentence, remarked means

    Ⓐ   asked.

    Ⓑ   felt surprised.

    Ⓒ   said.

    Ⓓ   felt glad.

19. Spines <u>project</u> from the plant's stem. The spines

    Ⓐ   are flat.

    Ⓑ   hang down.

    Ⓒ   are falling out.

    Ⓓ   stick out.

20. I have a <u>complete</u> set of Laura Ingalls Wilder's books. I have

    Ⓐ   some of Wilder's books.

    Ⓑ   more than half of Wilder's books.

    Ⓒ   all of Wilder's books.

    Ⓓ   very few of Wilder's books.

21. The new park will <u>benefit</u> our whole community. It will

    Ⓐ   clean up the community.

    Ⓑ   be useful to the community.

    Ⓒ   organize the community.

    Ⓓ   make the community more crowded.

22. How does swimming help <u>develop</u> strong muscles?

    Ⓐ   by making muscles grow

    Ⓑ   by showing muscles off

    Ⓒ   by hiding muscles

    Ⓓ   by relaxing tense muscles

23. The new building is <u>complete</u>. The work on the building is

    Ⓐ   very well done.

    Ⓑ   poorly done.

    Ⓒ   finished.

    Ⓓ   planned.

24. What is a <u>master</u> plan?

    Ⓐ   a new plan

    Ⓑ   the main plan

    Ⓒ   someone who is good at planning

    Ⓓ   a silly plan

25. What is one <u>benefit</u> of reading?

    Ⓐ   Some books are too difficult for fourth graders.

    Ⓑ   Many five-year-olds can read.

    Ⓒ   Some people need glasses for reading.

    Ⓓ   Reading can help you learn new words.

26. Which is a <u>patriotic</u> action?

    Ⓐ   pledging allegiance to the flag

    Ⓑ   having fun on weekends

    Ⓒ   planting a garden

    Ⓓ   completing math problems

27. What does the symbol $ <u>represent</u>?

    Ⓐ   capital *s*

    Ⓑ   dollar

    Ⓒ   senior

    Ⓓ   street

28. How do you <u>develop</u> photographs?

    Ⓐ   by displaying them in a photo album

    Ⓑ   by applying chemicals to photographic film

    Ⓒ   by taking pictures of interesting scenes

    Ⓓ   by choosing only the best photos for display

29. Which of the following might <u>dismay</u> someone?

    Ⓐ   a surprise birthday gift from a family member

    Ⓑ   news that a forest fire has started nearby

    Ⓒ   a long, slow walk down a country road

    Ⓓ   an exciting movie or television show

30. How might someone show <u>patriotism</u>?

    Ⓐ   by getting enough exercise

    Ⓑ   by teaching children to read

    Ⓒ   by voting in elections

    Ⓓ   by getting to school on time

31. Jane's phone call <u>eased</u> her mother's mind. How did the phone call make her mother feel?

    Ⓐ   less troubled

    Ⓑ   less angry

    Ⓒ   more unhappy

    Ⓓ   more excited

32. If it is <u>hailing</u> outside, what should you do?

    Ⓐ   go to the beach

    Ⓑ   lock the door

    Ⓒ   shut the windows

    Ⓓ   turn on the air conditioning

33. A mosquito bit Darryl's leg, and an itchy bump <u>developed.</u> What does <u>developed</u> mean in this sentence?

    Ⓐ   started to itch

    Ⓑ   appeared

    Ⓒ   became painful

    Ⓓ   turned red

34. What is a <u>lack</u> of rain?

    Ⓐ   a puddle

    Ⓑ   a shortage of rain

    Ⓒ   enough rain

    Ⓓ   a rain shower

35. If Seth <u>lacks</u> friends, what should he do?

    Ⓐ   phone his friends

    Ⓑ   send e-mail messages to his friends

    Ⓒ   try to make new friends

    Ⓓ   plan some activities to do with his friends

Name: _____   Date: _____

Book 4, Lesson 2 Test

Choose the BEST way to complete each sentence or answer each question. Then fill in the circle next to your answer.

1. A <u>grove</u> has rows of

   Ⓐ houses.

   Ⓑ chairs.

   Ⓒ trees.

   Ⓓ marchers.

2. Which means the same as <u>permit</u>?

   Ⓐ allow

   Ⓑ scold

   Ⓒ insist

   Ⓓ command

3. <u>Excessive</u> spending is

   Ⓐ money for clothing.

   Ⓑ spending too much.

   Ⓒ saving a little money.

   Ⓓ money for groceries.

4. Which of these <u>affect</u> the weather?

   Ⓐ houses

   Ⓑ picnics

   Ⓒ warm sweaters

   Ⓓ the seasons

5. To <u>calculate</u> an answer, you use

   Ⓐ a dictionary.

   Ⓑ an encyclopedia.

   Ⓒ a secret code.

   Ⓓ math.

6. Which describes a desert's <u>climate</u>?

    Ⓐ   hot and dry

    Ⓑ   a cactus with sharp spines

    Ⓒ   rattlesnakes and kangaroo rats

    Ⓓ   sandy soil with few trees

7. Alex <u>scorched</u> his grilled cheese sandwich. What does this mean?

    Ⓐ   He cooked it slowly.

    Ⓑ   He burnt it slightly.

    Ⓒ   He ate it quickly.

    Ⓓ   He shared it with his friend.

8. A <u>towering</u> figure is one that is

    Ⓐ   slender.

    Ⓑ   hard to recognize.

    Ⓒ   shadowy.

    Ⓓ   very tall.

9. To <u>resist</u> a new rule is to

    Ⓐ   ask people to follow it.

    Ⓑ   get used to it.

    Ⓒ   fight against it.

    Ⓓ   obey it.

10. Which part of a tree is a <u>limb</u>?

    Ⓐ   a branch

    Ⓑ   a leaf

    Ⓒ   a trunk

    Ⓓ   a root

11. How can you prevent tooth <u>decay</u>?

    Ⓐ   by smiling often

    Ⓑ   by eating candy

    Ⓒ   by exercising regularly

    Ⓓ   by brushing your teeth regularly

12. The actor <u>affects</u> an English accent. This means that he

    Ⓐ   speaks with a pretend English accent.

    Ⓑ   speaks with an English accent because he is English.

    Ⓒ   can't understand people who speak with English accents.

    Ⓓ   loves listening to English accents.

13. To <u>calculate</u> the risk of an accident is to

    Ⓐ   use reason to figure out whether an accident is likely.

    Ⓑ   add and subtract to figure out whether an accident is likely.

    Ⓒ   predict that an accident will surely happen.

    Ⓓ   have no fear of an accident.

14. A newspaper <u>column</u> is

    Ⓐ   a reporter.

    Ⓑ   a delivery route.

    Ⓒ   an article that appears regularly.

    Ⓓ   an advertisement that appears regularly.

15. What do stone <u>columns</u> do?

    Ⓐ   support buildings

    Ⓑ   lie in streambeds

    Ⓒ   are huge boulders

    Ⓓ   form walkways

16. Dad painted the house and told Luis that he could use the <u>excess</u> paint. What did Dad do?

    Ⓐ   let Luis help him paint the house

    Ⓑ   let Luis use the extra paint

    Ⓒ   let Luis have the paintbrushes

    Ⓓ   let Luis use all the paint he wanted

17. After the kitten <u>matures</u>, it will be

    Ⓐ   clean and fluffy.

    Ⓑ   a cat.

    Ⓒ   full of cat food.

    Ⓓ   purring happily.

18. Which of these <u>resists</u> rain?

    Ⓐ   a daisy

    Ⓑ   a pair of socks

    Ⓒ   a raincoat

    Ⓓ   soil

19. Which amount <u>exceeds</u> one cup?

    Ⓐ   1/2 cup

    Ⓑ   1/4 cup

    Ⓒ   1 gallon

    Ⓓ   1 teaspoon

20. Kai has powerful <u>limbs</u>. This means that he

    Ⓐ   is a talented artist.

    Ⓑ   is very intelligent.

    Ⓒ   has excellent eyesight.

    Ⓓ   has strong arms and legs.

21. Which is a <u>column</u> of names?

    Ⓐ   Annie, Ben, Carlos, Dee

    Ⓑ   Annie

           Ben

           Carlos

           Dee

    Ⓒ Annie

           Ben

               Carlos

                  Dee

    Ⓓ   Annie, Ben, Carlos, Lee, Carlos Perez, and Dee Johnson

22. To <u>decay</u> is to

    Ⓐ   shine.

    Ⓑ   burn.

    Ⓒ   rot.

    Ⓓ   fail.

23. Which two words have OPPOSITE meanings?

    Ⓐ   forbid and exceed

    Ⓑ   forbid and permit

    Ⓒ   affect and decay

    Ⓓ   climate and scorching

24. To exceed the speed limit is to

    Ⓐ   drive faster than the speed limit.

    Ⓑ   drive at a safe speed.

    Ⓒ   post the speed limit on a sign.

    Ⓓ   be aware of the speed limit.

25. Which of these requires a permit?

    Ⓐ   walking to school

    Ⓑ   driving a car

    Ⓒ   doing homework

    Ⓓ   eating lunch in the cafeteria

26. Which of these is most likely to tower over a person?

    Ⓐ   a table

    Ⓑ   a dog

    Ⓒ   a skyscraper

    Ⓓ   a car

For items 27–30, find the word that means the OPPOSITE of the underlined word. Then fill in the circle next to your answer.

27. mature

    Ⓐ   fearful

    Ⓑ   sluggish

    Ⓒ   young

    Ⓓ   quiet

28. mammoth

    Ⓐ   tiny

    Ⓑ   beautiful

    Ⓒ   smooth

    Ⓓ   shiny

29. <u>scorching</u>

      Ⓐ   freezing

      Ⓑ   drenched

      Ⓒ   comfortable

      Ⓓ   peaceful

30. <u>forbidden</u>

      Ⓐ   bright

      Ⓑ   ordinary

      Ⓒ   permitted

      Ⓓ   joyful

Book 4, Lesson 3 Test

Choose the BEST way to complete each sentence or answer each question. Then fill in the circle next to your answer.

1. To <u>approach</u> New York City is to

   Ⓐ   live there.

   Ⓑ   work there.

   Ⓒ   go closer to New York City.

   Ⓓ   completely surround New York City.

2. To feel <u>drowsy</u> is to feel

   Ⓐ   hungry.

   Ⓑ   sleepy.

   Ⓒ   thirsty.

   Ⓓ   bored.

3. Someone who is <u>famished</u> is

   Ⓐ   very tired.

   Ⓑ   very intelligent.

   Ⓒ   very hungry.

   Ⓓ   very sad.

4. Which word means about the same as <u>forecast</u>?

   Ⓐ   predict

   Ⓑ   wonder

   Ⓒ   question

   Ⓓ   command

5. Which of these describes an <u>approach</u>?

   Ⓐ   a driveway leading up to a house

   Ⓑ   a large house in the middle of a lawn

   Ⓒ   a small playground

   Ⓓ   a fenced yard

6. When birds <u>migrate</u>, they

- Ⓐ lay eggs.
- Ⓑ fish in marshy areas.
- Ⓒ fly from one region to another.
- Ⓓ choose mates and build their nests.

7. To <u>nestle</u> in an armchair is to

- Ⓐ sit up straight.
- Ⓑ curl up comfortably.
- Ⓒ read an interesting book.
- Ⓓ share the chair with another person.

8. Which means the OPPOSITE of <u>cease</u>?

- Ⓐ begin
- Ⓑ stay
- Ⓒ try
- Ⓓ help

9. <u>Severe</u> weather is

- Ⓐ sunny and breezy.
- Ⓑ cool and cloudy.
- Ⓒ difficult to deal with.
- Ⓓ suitable for a picnic.

10. To <u>venture</u> outside is to

- Ⓐ dare to go outside.
- Ⓑ play happily in an outdoor spot.
- Ⓒ be afraid of going outside.
- Ⓓ have a picnic outside.

11. To <u>burrow</u> through a stack of magazines is to

- Ⓐ place the magazines in a neat pile.
- Ⓑ sort the magazines into groups.
- Ⓒ search through the magazines.
- Ⓓ flip lazily through the pages.

12. The store manager plans to <u>reduce</u> his staff. He plans to

    Ⓐ   train his workers.

    Ⓑ   treat his workers fairly.

    Ⓒ   have fewer workers on his staff.

    Ⓓ   be more strict with his workers.

13. To <u>observe</u> the speed limit is to

    Ⓐ   know how fast the speed limit is.

    Ⓑ   notice a speed limit sign.

    Ⓒ   obey the speed limit.

    Ⓓ   argue that the speed limit should be faster.

14. To <u>observe</u> Thanksgiving Day is to

    Ⓐ   celebrate it.

    Ⓑ   learn its history.

    Ⓒ   remind others that it is coming soon.

    Ⓓ   go to work or school on Thanksgiving Day.

15. The <u>approach</u> of spring is

    Ⓐ   the middle of spring.

    Ⓑ   the way people feel during springtime.

    Ⓒ   when spring is coming.

    Ⓓ   the way animals behave during springtime.

16. A <u>destructive</u> storm is

    Ⓐ   a rainstorm.

    Ⓑ   a snowstorm.

    Ⓒ   one that causes damage.

    Ⓓ   one that is unexpected.

17. What is a price <u>reduction</u>?

    Ⓐ   a lower price

    Ⓑ   a higher price

    Ⓒ   a way of keeping track of prices

    Ⓓ   a way of figuring out how much items should cost

18. To <u>observe</u> a wild animal is to

  Ⓐ keep a safe distance from it.

  Ⓑ watch it.

  Ⓒ protect it.

  Ⓓ hunt for it.

19. A <u>migratory</u> animal is one that

  Ⓐ mates for life.

  Ⓑ eats only vegetables.

  Ⓒ lays eggs.

  Ⓓ moves from one place to another.

20. <u>Migration</u> is the act of

  Ⓐ leaving primary school to go to middle school.

  Ⓑ suffering from a headache.

  Ⓒ moving from one region or country to another.

  Ⓓ graduating from high school.

21. "We'll be late for school," Pia <u>observed</u>. In this sentence, <u>observed</u> means

  Ⓐ complained.

  Ⓑ remarked.

  Ⓒ predicted.

  Ⓓ shouted.

22. Which phrase describes <u>destruction</u>?

  Ⓐ a flood

  Ⓑ homes ruined by flood waters

  Ⓒ a sudden, heavy rainstorm

  Ⓓ workers rescuing flood victims

23. A business <u>venture</u> always involves

  Ⓐ a large number of people.

  Ⓑ great success.

  Ⓒ a new store or restaurant.

  Ⓓ a risk.

24. Which phrase describes party <u>preparations</u>?

    Ⓐ   making sandwiches for a party

    Ⓑ   dancing at a party

    Ⓒ   playing music at a party

    Ⓓ   laughing and talking at a party

25. A weather <u>forecast</u> is

    Ⓐ   an area's climate.

    Ⓑ   a TV weather person.

    Ⓒ   a weather prediction.

    Ⓓ   a bad storm.

26. Which of these is most likely to live in a <u>burrow</u>?

    Ⓐ   a horse

    Ⓑ   an elephant

    Ⓒ   a rabbit

    Ⓓ   a fourth-grade student

27. Which word is closest in meaning to <u>severe</u>?

    Ⓐ   sorrowful

    Ⓑ   harsh

    Ⓒ   unusual

    Ⓓ   eerie

28. When a bear <u>hibernates</u>, it

    Ⓐ   sheds its winter coat.

    Ⓑ   spends the winter resting.

    Ⓒ   spends the summer storing body fat.

    Ⓓ   defends its cubs.

29. Where might a town be <u>nestled</u>?

    Ⓐ   in a hidden valley

    Ⓑ   on top of a hill

    Ⓒ   on an open plain

    Ⓓ   on a wide, flat desert landscape

30. Which of these <u>burrows</u> into the earth?

     Ⓐ   a rock

     Ⓑ   a mole

     Ⓒ   a leaf

     Ⓓ   a lake

31. To <u>prepare</u> for a party is to

     Ⓐ   enjoy it very much.

     Ⓑ   get ready for it.

     Ⓒ   tell others how much fun it was.

     Ⓓ   ask permission to have a party.

32. Which word means about the same as <u>forecast</u>?

     Ⓐ   command

     Ⓑ   wonder

     Ⓒ   question

     Ⓓ   predict

Name: _____ Date: _____

Book 4, Lesson 4 Test

Choose the BEST way to complete each sentence or answer each question. Then fill in the circle next to your answer.

1. To <u>attend</u> a meeting is to

   Ⓐ lead it.

   Ⓑ go to it.

   Ⓒ plan it.

   Ⓓ end it.

2. <u>Astounding</u> news is

   Ⓐ sad news.

   Ⓑ joyful news.

   Ⓒ very surprising news.

   Ⓓ information that someone already knows.

3. A <u>modest</u> home is

   Ⓐ a large, beautiful one.

   Ⓑ one that is located outside of a city.

   Ⓒ a temporary one.

   Ⓓ a simple one.

4. A <u>grace</u> period is

   Ⓐ about a week.

   Ⓑ extra time to get something done.

   Ⓒ a vacation.

   Ⓓ a period before a holiday.

5. To say <u>grace</u> is to

   Ⓐ say a prayer before a meal.

   Ⓑ say a prayer at bedtime.

   Ⓒ make a promise to someone.

   Ⓓ sign a contract.

6. The swan moves with <u>grace</u>. This means that it

    Ⓐ   moves slowly.

    Ⓑ   moves beautifully.

    Ⓒ   moves in a sneaky way.

    Ⓓ   has jerky movements.

7. <u>Paralysis</u> means not being able to

    Ⓐ   speak.

    Ⓑ   hear.

    Ⓒ   see.

    Ⓓ   move.

8. <u>Parallel</u> stories are

    Ⓐ   fairytales.

    Ⓑ   similar.

    Ⓒ   unbelievable.

    Ⓓ   boring.

9. To <u>impose</u> on someone is to

    Ⓐ   take unfair advantage of that person.

    Ⓑ   argue with that person.

    Ⓒ   command that person to do something.

    Ⓓ   chase that person.

10. Mr. Klein signed a <u>contract</u> with his partner. A <u>contract</u> is

    Ⓐ   an e-mail message.

    Ⓑ   a friendly letter.

    Ⓒ   a greeting card.

    Ⓓ   a lawful agreement.

11. Dr. Kim <u>contracted</u> chicken pox. This means that he

    Ⓐ   treated a patient with chicken pox.

    Ⓑ   became ill with chicken pox.

    Ⓒ   discovered a cure for chicken pox.

    Ⓓ   infected another person with chicken pox.

12. Ms. Leigh <u>contracted</u> painters to paint the room. This means that she

    Ⓐ   made a legal agreement with the painters.

    Ⓑ   had a phone conversation with the painters.

    Ⓒ   helped the painters with their work.

    Ⓓ   asked the painters to hurry.

13. Leona <u>cherished</u> her new sister. This means that Leona

    Ⓐ   was jealous of her sister.

    Ⓑ   looked like her sister.

    Ⓒ   welcomed her sister.

    Ⓓ   loved her sister.

14. Mr. Westfall <u>cherishes</u> the idea that his lost dog will return. In this sentence, <u>cherishes</u> means

    Ⓐ   clings to.

    Ⓑ   dislikes.

    Ⓒ   remembers.

    Ⓓ   forgets.

15. To <u>attend</u> to your homework is to

    Ⓐ   forget it at school.

    Ⓑ   ask questions about it.

    Ⓒ   pay attention to it.

    Ⓓ   refuse to do it.

16. A piano <u>recital</u> is a

    Ⓐ   class.

    Ⓑ   player.

    Ⓒ   song.

    Ⓓ   performance.

17. Jonathan has an <u>active</u> imagination. His imagination is

    Ⓐ   normal.

    Ⓑ   unusual.

    Ⓒ   lively.

    Ⓓ   creative.

18. Julie was an <u>active</u> participant in our discussion. She

    Ⓐ   listened carefully but did not talk.

    Ⓑ   was not there during the discussion.

    Ⓒ   seemed bored during the discussion.

    Ⓓ   took part in the discussion.

19. "I'm fine, thanks," she <u>responded</u>. In this sentence, <u>responded</u> means

    Ⓐ   answered.

    Ⓑ   snapped.

    Ⓒ   commented.

    Ⓓ   whispered.

20. To <u>expose</u> a secret plan is to

    Ⓐ   complete it.

    Ⓑ   ask about it.

    Ⓒ   make it known.

    Ⓓ   think about it.

21. The hole in the rug <u>exposed</u> the wood floor. In this sentence, <u>exposed</u> means

    Ⓐ   ruined.

    Ⓑ   scratched.

    Ⓒ   dulled.

    Ⓓ   showed.

22. What does it mean if you <u>expose</u> film to sunlight?

    Ⓐ   You fail to protect it from the sun.

    Ⓑ   You take pictures of sunny landscapes.

    Ⓒ   You take pictures of dark landscapes.

    Ⓓ   You fail to keep the film warm.

23. To <u>impose</u> new rules is to

    Ⓐ   discuss them.

    Ⓑ   plan them.

    Ⓒ   force people to follow them.

    Ⓓ   beg people to follow them.

24. To <u>recite</u> a poem is to

    Ⓐ   write a poem.

    Ⓑ   say a poem aloud to others.

    Ⓒ   read a poem silently to yourself.

    Ⓓ   figure out what a poem means.

25. To <u>contract</u> is to

    Ⓐ   go higher.

    Ⓑ   sit motionless.

    Ⓒ   move quickly.

    Ⓓ   grow smaller.

26. Which is a <u>response</u> to "How are you?"

    Ⓐ   "How are you?"

    Ⓑ   "Hello."

    Ⓒ   "I'm fine, thank you."

    Ⓓ   "I'm eleven years old."

27. Which of these hobbies is most <u>active</u>?

    Ⓐ   playing chess

    Ⓑ   playing soccer

    Ⓒ   reading

    Ⓓ   collecting baseball cards

28. Which of these is most likely to <u>astound</u> someone?

    Ⓐ   playing in the schoolyard with friends

    Ⓑ   crawling into a sleeping bag after a long day's hike

    Ⓒ   eating a peanut butter sandwich

    Ⓓ   watching an acrobat do an amazing stunt

29. Which sounds like something a <u>pessimist</u> might say?

    Ⓐ   "What a nice day!"

    Ⓑ   "I'm sure it will rain. Our picnic will be ruined!"

    Ⓒ   "I'm sure it will clear up soon."

    Ⓓ   "Let's listen to the weather report."

30. Which sounds like something a <u>modest</u> person might say?

Ⓐ   "Thanks, but Angelo deserves all the credit."

Ⓑ   "Thanks. It's true that I worked very hard on the project."

Ⓒ   "Yes, we did a great job!"

Ⓓ   "Angelo helped a little, but I did most of the work."

31. Which is an example of <u>parallel</u> lines?

Ⓐ   X

Ⓑ   =

Ⓒ   +

Ⓓ   T

32. Which of these is most likely to <u>paralyze</u> a small animal?

Ⓐ   food

Ⓑ   warmth

Ⓒ   fear

Ⓓ   curiosity

33. Which of these is most likely to <u>paralyze</u> a city?

Ⓐ   a celebration

Ⓑ   stores and restaurants

Ⓒ   a blizzard

Ⓓ   sunny weather

For items 34–36, find the word that means the OPPOSITE of the underlined word. Then fill in the circle next to your answer.

34. <u>eager</u>

Ⓐ   generous

Ⓑ   serious

Ⓒ   curious

Ⓓ   unwilling

35. <u>modesty</u>

Ⓐ   generosity

Ⓑ   pride

Ⓒ   malice

Ⓓ   injury

36. <u>graceful</u>

    Ⓐ   clumsy

    Ⓑ   fearful

    Ⓒ   selfish

    Ⓓ   harmful

For items 37–38, find the word that means about the SAME as the underlined word. Then fill in the circle next to your answer.

37. <u>eagerly</u>

    Ⓐ   thoughtfully

    Ⓑ   sleepily

    Ⓒ   enthusiastically

    Ⓓ   sorrowfully

38. <u>pessimistic</u>

    Ⓐ   gloomy

    Ⓑ   curious

    Ⓒ   exhausted

    Ⓓ   interested

Book 4, Lesson 5 Test

Choose the BEST way to complete each sentence or answer each question. Then fill in the circle next to your answer.

1. To <u>mock</u> someone is to

   Ⓐ argue with that person.

   Ⓑ make fun of that person.

   Ⓒ follow that person.

   Ⓓ lead that person.

2. The OPPOSITE of <u>contempt</u> is

   Ⓐ curiosity.

   Ⓑ happiness.

   Ⓒ surprise.

   Ⓓ admiration.

3. To <u>persist</u> is to

   Ⓐ bother someone.

   Ⓑ keep on trying.

   Ⓒ sweat.

   Ⓓ act finicky.

4. To <u>entertain</u> a child is to

   Ⓐ keep him or her amused.

   Ⓑ teach him or her to read.

   Ⓒ carry him or her.

   Ⓓ talk to him or her.

5. Ty is <u>entertaining</u> the idea of running for class president. What is Ty doing?

   Ⓐ He has decided not to run for president.

   Ⓑ He is thinking about running for president.

   Ⓒ He thinks his friend should run for president.

   Ⓓ He does not want to have a class president.

6. To <u>entertain</u> friends is to

    Ⓐ   have them as guests.

    Ⓑ   make new friends.

    Ⓒ   keep in touch with them.

    Ⓓ   get to know them.

7. What is a <u>glimpse</u>?

    Ⓐ   a quick nap.

    Ⓑ   a short trip.

    Ⓒ   a small snack.

    Ⓓ   a quick look.

8. To <u>attempt</u> is to

    Ⓐ   fail.

    Ⓑ   try.

    Ⓒ   win.

    Ⓓ   argue.

9. The baby made an <u>attempt</u> to stand up. An <u>attempt</u> is

    Ⓐ   an effort.

    Ⓑ   a request.

    Ⓒ   a movement.

    Ⓓ   a success.

10. To <u>achieve</u> a goal is to

    Ⓐ   set a goal.

    Ⓑ   reach a goal.

    Ⓒ   try to reach a goal.

    Ⓓ   cheer when a soccer player scores.

11. To <u>glimpse</u> at a book is to

    Ⓐ   write a book.

    Ⓑ   read a book.

    Ⓒ   take a quick look at a book.

    Ⓓ   borrow a book from the library.

12. Someone with <u>persistence</u> does NOT

    Ⓐ make unkind comments.

    Ⓑ behave politely.

    Ⓒ give up easily.

    Ⓓ use teamwork.

13. I hope this cool weather <u>persists</u>. In this sentence, <u>persists</u> means

    Ⓐ stops after a while.

    Ⓑ becomes warmer.

    Ⓒ stops right away.

    Ⓓ goes on and on.

14. "Wow!" said Ronnie in <u>mock</u> surprise. In this sentence, <u>mock</u> means

    Ⓐ shocked.

    Ⓑ pretend.

    Ⓒ great.

    Ⓓ mild.

15. A <u>sensitive</u> person is

    Ⓐ a talented artist.

    Ⓑ in poor health.

    Ⓒ quick to feel an emotion.

    Ⓓ skilled at math.

16. To <u>recall</u> a song is to

    Ⓐ listen to it on the radio.

    Ⓑ sing it.

    Ⓒ like it very much.

    Ⓓ remember it.

17. A factory <u>reject</u> is a product that is

    Ⓐ popular.

    Ⓑ cheap.

    Ⓒ attractive.

    Ⓓ unacceptable.

18. To <u>revise</u> an encyclopedia is to

- Ⓐ find information in it.
- Ⓑ read it for pleasure.
- Ⓒ bring it up to date.
- Ⓓ place it on a bookshelf.

19. Which of these might someone <u>revise</u>?

- Ⓐ a story
- Ⓑ an apple
- Ⓒ a baby
- Ⓓ a tree

20. Why might a food manufacturing company <u>recall</u> one of its products?

- Ⓐ because the product is delicious
- Ⓑ because the product is popular
- Ⓒ because the product is useful
- Ⓓ because the product is unsafe

21. Which might be described as <u>quaint</u>?

- Ⓐ a skyscraper built in 2002
- Ⓑ clothing from the 1920s
- Ⓒ a grizzly bear
- Ⓓ a lake surrounded by trees

22. Which means about the same as <u>persuade</u>?

- Ⓐ apologize
- Ⓑ convince
- Ⓒ explain
- Ⓓ comfort

23. Which of these is meant to be <u>persuasive</u>?

- Ⓐ facts about wild animals
- Ⓑ a story with talking animal characters
- Ⓒ a TV commercial for a toy store
- Ⓓ a sign that gives the speed limit

24. Which is one <u>phase</u> of a frog's life?

  Ⓐ breathing through its skin

  Ⓑ the tadpole stage

  Ⓒ taking long leaps

  Ⓓ eating flies

25. Which of these describes an <u>achievement</u>?

  Ⓐ graduating from middle school

  Ⓑ a high school building

  Ⓒ a middle school teacher

  Ⓓ an elementary school student

26. Which is a <u>persistent</u> collector most likely to do?

  Ⓐ steal someone else's baseball cards

  Ⓑ give baseball cards to others as gifts

  Ⓒ keep collecting baseball cards

  Ⓓ lose interest in collecting baseball cards

27. Which of these might be <u>sensitive</u> to sunlight?

  Ⓐ a rock

  Ⓑ a person's skin

  Ⓒ a stone building

  Ⓓ a sidewalk

28. Which means about the same as <u>abrupt</u>?

  Ⓐ rude

  Ⓑ sudden

  Ⓒ odd

  Ⓓ unkind

29. Which means the OPPOSITE of <u>reject</u>?

  Ⓐ accept

  Ⓑ cheer up

  Ⓒ lighten

  Ⓓ question

Book 4, Lesson 6 Test

Choose the BEST way to complete each sentence or answer each question. Then fill in the circle next to your answer.

1. When you <u>disclose</u> information, you

   Ⓐ tell people about it.

   Ⓑ learn about it on TV.

   Ⓒ invent it.

   Ⓓ read about it in a newspaper.

2. An <u>exquisite</u> necklace is

   Ⓐ old-fashioned.

   Ⓑ colorful.

   Ⓒ beautifully made.

   Ⓓ glittery.

3. I <u>intend</u> to leave in the morning. In this sentence, <u>intend</u> means

   Ⓐ plan.

   Ⓑ hope.

   Ⓒ hate.

   Ⓓ request permission.

4. Jackie ate the <u>entire</u> pizza. In this sentence, <u>entire</u> means

   Ⓐ whole.

   Ⓑ delicious.

   Ⓒ medium-sized.

   Ⓓ messy.

5. If you ask <u>in vain</u>, you

   Ⓐ ask angrily.

   Ⓑ feel certain that you will get what you asked for.

   Ⓒ don't get what you asked for.

   Ⓓ beg for something.

6. We watched John's <u>progress</u> up the road. In this sentence, <u>progress</u> means

    Ⓐ   moving toward a goal.

    Ⓑ   car.

    Ⓒ   bicycle.

    Ⓓ   moving in a wavy line.

7. If construction work on a new building <u>progresses</u>, it

    Ⓐ   is impressive.

    Ⓑ   moves forward.

    Ⓒ   takes a long time.

    Ⓓ   makes a lot of noise.

8. Jerome had no <u>intention</u> of hurting Kate's feelings. In this sentence, <u>intention</u> means

    Ⓐ   aim or plan.

    Ⓑ   responsibility.

    Ⓒ   trouble.

    Ⓓ   guilt.

9. If you make <u>progress</u>, you

    Ⓐ   irritate people.

    Ⓑ   do your work slowly.

    Ⓒ   try as hard as you can.

    Ⓓ   make an improvement.

10. To <u>refine</u> sugar is to

    Ⓐ   enjoy sugary desserts.

    Ⓑ   avoid eating sugar.

    Ⓒ   use sugar for cooking.

    Ⓓ   purify sugar.

11. We made a <u>vain</u> attempt to find the key. This means

    Ⓐ   we tried, but could not find the key.

    Ⓑ   we did our best and succeeded at last.

    Ⓒ   we are still looking for the key.

    Ⓓ   we did not try very hard to find the key.

12. Which of these is <u>refined</u>?

    Ⓐ   corn on the cob

    Ⓑ   pure white flour

    Ⓒ   a head of lettuce

    Ⓓ   a wheat plant

13. Which of these is someone most likely to <u>exclaim</u>?

    Ⓐ   "What a beautiful day!"

    Ⓑ   "Please join us for breakfast."

    Ⓒ   "May I have some orange juice?"

    Ⓓ   "I'm going shopping tomorrow."

14. Which of the following can be a <u>scoundrel</u>?

    Ⓐ   a business person

    Ⓑ   a bus passenger

    Ⓒ   a bank robber

    Ⓓ   a pet cat

15. Which is an <u>exclamation</u>?

    Ⓐ   "I'm fine, thank you."

    Ⓑ   "Ouch!"

    Ⓒ   "Please pass the salt."

    Ⓓ   "How are you?"

16. What are <u>jeers</u> meant to do?

    Ⓐ   to praise someone

    Ⓑ   to warn someone of danger

    Ⓒ   to insult or mock someone

    Ⓓ   ask politely for silence

17. What would an animal use to <u>peer</u> at you?

    Ⓐ   its fangs

    Ⓑ   its eyes

    Ⓒ   its claws

    Ⓓ   its voice

18. Which describes <u>applause</u>?

    Ⓐ   running and jumping

    Ⓑ   clapping and cheering

    Ⓒ   whining and complaining

    Ⓓ   whispering secrets

19. Who or what is most likely to <u>applaud</u>?

    Ⓐ   animals in a forest

    Ⓑ   flowers in a garden

    Ⓒ   people in an audience

    Ⓓ   people hurrying along a sidewalk

For items 20-22, find the word that means the OPPOSITE of the underlined word. Then fill in the circle next to your answer.

20. <u>refined</u>

    Ⓐ   rude

    Ⓑ   wealthy

    Ⓒ   hungry

    Ⓓ   exhausted

21. <u>vain</u>

    Ⓐ   beautiful

    Ⓑ   modest

    Ⓒ   loving

    Ⓓ   generous

22. <u>drab</u>

    Ⓐ   sad

    Ⓑ   colorful

    Ⓒ   kind

    Ⓓ   moist

For items 23-26, find the word that means about the SAME as the underlined word. Then fill in the circle next to your answer.

23. <u>crafty</u>

     Ⓐ   sneaky

     Ⓑ   intelligent

     Ⓒ   curious

     Ⓓ   furious

24. <u>jeer</u>

     Ⓐ   greet

     Ⓑ   cheer

     Ⓒ   mock

     Ⓓ   wave

25. <u>progress</u>

     Ⓐ   contract

     Ⓑ   improve

     Ⓒ   shrink

     Ⓓ   age

26. <u>uneasy</u>

     Ⓐ   exhausted

     Ⓑ   angry

     Ⓒ   nervous

     Ⓓ   curious

Book 4, Lesson 7 Test

Choose the BEST way to complete each sentence or answer each question. Then fill in the circle next to your answer.

1. An <u>alteration</u> is a

   Ⓐ surprise.

   Ⓑ habit.

   Ⓒ change.

   Ⓓ plan.

2. The homework assignment <u>confused</u> me. It

   Ⓐ bored me.

   Ⓑ wasn't clear to me.

   Ⓒ interested me.

   Ⓓ was easy for me to complete.

3. On the telephone it's possible to <u>confuse</u> the names John and Shaun. In this sentence, <u>confuse</u> means

   Ⓐ say very loudly.

   Ⓑ say very quickly.

   Ⓒ mistake one for the other.

   Ⓓ hear very clearly.

4. To <u>distribute</u> snacks is to

   Ⓐ eat them.

   Ⓑ buy them.

   Ⓒ give them out.

   Ⓓ throw them away.

5. To <u>embrace</u> an idea is to

   Ⓐ invent it.

   Ⓑ question it.

   Ⓒ take it seriously.

   Ⓓ understand it.

6. The art teacher <u>equipped</u> us with paints and brushes. To <u>equip</u> is to

   Ⓐ   request.

   Ⓑ   borrow.

   Ⓒ   buy.

   Ⓓ   provide what is needed.

7. Recycle bins are <u>distributed</u> throughout the school. In this sentence, <u>distributed</u> means

   Ⓐ   spread out.

   Ⓑ   filled.

   Ⓒ   empty.

   Ⓓ   stacked.

8. To be <u>flexible</u> is to be able to

   Ⓐ   get to school on time.

   Ⓑ   adjust to new situations.

   Ⓒ   plan activities.

   Ⓓ   predict what will happen.

9. What is a <u>limp</u>?

   Ⓐ   a fast gallop

   Ⓑ   a quick trot

   Ⓒ   a ballet dance

   Ⓓ   an uneven walk

10. To <u>seize</u> someone's hand is to

   Ⓐ   grab it suddenly.

   Ⓑ   slap it.

   Ⓒ   stroke it.

   Ⓓ   hold it gently.

11. A <u>shallow</u> conversation is one that

   Ⓐ   involves many people.

   Ⓑ   is not very serious.

   Ⓒ   involves only two people.

   Ⓓ   is a secret.

12. A school's <u>surroundings</u> are

    Ⓐ   its students.

    Ⓑ   its teachers.

    Ⓒ   the buildings and trees around it.

    Ⓓ   its sports teams.

13. Which of these can <u>surround</u> a house?

    Ⓐ   a window

    Ⓑ   a door

    Ⓒ   a kitchen

    Ⓓ   a fence

14. Which of these is a <u>victim</u>?

    Ⓐ   stolen money

    Ⓑ   a police officer who catches a thief

    Ⓒ   someone whose money is stolen

    Ⓓ   a thief

15. Who might <u>seize</u> stolen television sets?

    Ⓐ   a store that sells television sets

    Ⓑ   the people who own them

    Ⓒ   thieves

    Ⓓ   police officers

16. Which of these is most likely to <u>scurry</u>?

    Ⓐ   a horse

    Ⓑ   a mouse

    Ⓒ   an elephant

    Ⓓ   a whale

17. Which could be described as <u>keen</u>?

    Ⓐ   a person's foot

    Ⓑ   a person's hair

    Ⓒ   a person's brain

    Ⓓ   a person's hand

18. Who or what is most likely to <u>limp</u>?

    Ⓐ   a woman who has broken her arm

    Ⓑ   an excited dog

    Ⓒ   a snake

    Ⓓ   a man who has injured his foot

19. Which of these could be described as <u>keen</u>?

    Ⓐ   a spoon

    Ⓑ   a plate

    Ⓒ   a knife

    Ⓓ   a place mat

20. Which of these takes only an <u>instant</u>?

    Ⓐ   doing your homework

    Ⓑ   glancing at the clock

    Ⓒ   walking to school

    Ⓓ   eating lunch

21. Which of these is most <u>flexible</u>?

    Ⓐ   a wooden ruler

    Ⓑ   a fork

    Ⓒ   a table

    Ⓓ   a rubber band

22. Which of these are sports <u>equipment</u>?

    Ⓐ   baseball players

    Ⓑ   baseball fields

    Ⓒ   gloves, balls, and bats

    Ⓓ   baseball coaches

23. Who or what is most likely to give you an <u>embrace</u>?

    Ⓐ   a dog

    Ⓑ   your home

    Ⓒ   the mail carrier

    Ⓓ   your grandmother

24. Which is a good reason for <u>ejecting</u> a student from the classroom?

    Ⓐ   The student is absent because of illness.

    Ⓑ   The student asks good questions.

    Ⓒ   The student turns in her homework on time.

    Ⓓ   The student disrupts the class.

For items 25–28, find the word that means about the SAME as the underlined word. Then fill in the circle next to your answer.

25. <u>embrace</u>

    Ⓐ   kiss

    Ⓑ   hug

    Ⓒ   greet

    Ⓓ   salute

26. <u>alter</u>

    Ⓐ   change

    Ⓑ   improve

    Ⓒ   harm

    Ⓓ   organize

27. <u>keen</u>

    Ⓐ   calm

    Ⓑ   gentle

    Ⓒ   musical

    Ⓓ   eager

28. <u>confusion</u>

    Ⓐ   anger

    Ⓑ   sorrow

    Ⓒ   disorder

    Ⓓ   haste

For items 29–32, find the word that means the OPPOSITE of the underlined word. Then fill in the circle next to your answer.

29. <u>instant</u>

    Ⓐ   bumpy

    Ⓑ   smooth

    Ⓒ   curved

    Ⓓ   slow

30. <u>limp</u>

    Ⓐ   firm

    Ⓑ   wrinkled

    Ⓒ   shiny

    Ⓓ   rough

31. <u>shallow</u>

    Ⓐ   wide

    Ⓑ   deep

    Ⓒ   plump

    Ⓓ   tall

32. <u>confusing</u>

    Ⓐ   sudden

    Ⓑ   gradual

    Ⓒ   clear

    Ⓓ   instant

Book 4, Lesson 8 Test

Choose the BEST way to complete each sentence or answer each question. Then fill in the circle next to your answer.

1. A <u>chamber</u> is a large

   Ⓐ house.

   Ⓑ lamp.

   Ⓒ room.

   Ⓓ yard.

2. An <u>ancient</u> city is very

   Ⓐ large.

   Ⓑ beautiful.

   Ⓒ strongly built.

   Ⓓ old.

3. A judge's <u>chambers</u> are

   Ⓐ her home.

   Ⓑ her courtroom.

   Ⓒ her office or offices.

   Ⓓ her assistants.

4. An <u>entry</u> is a way to get

   Ⓐ upstairs.

   Ⓑ downstairs.

   Ⓒ outside.

   Ⓓ inside.

5. To <u>intrude</u> is to go

   Ⓐ quickly.

   Ⓑ slowly.

   Ⓒ without permission.

   Ⓓ with caution.

6. Where will the city <u>locate</u> the new library? In this sentence, <u>locate</u> means

- Ⓐ to raise money for
- Ⓑ to advertise
- Ⓒ to find a place for
- Ⓓ to celebrate

7. A <u>passage</u> in a book is

- Ⓐ the book's cover.
- Ⓑ the book's author.
- Ⓒ part of the book.
- Ⓓ the book's illustrations.

8. The <u>passage</u> of time is

- Ⓐ a clock.
- Ⓑ a calendar.
- Ⓒ a kitchen timer.
- Ⓓ time going by.

9. A <u>precious</u> child is

- Ⓐ loved a lot.
- Ⓑ tired a lot.
- Ⓒ very intelligent.
- Ⓓ very imaginative.

10. What are hunters' <u>quarries</u>?

- Ⓐ their hunting season
- Ⓑ their hunting permits
- Ⓒ their clothing
- Ⓓ the animals that they are hunting

11. Joyce seemed happy on the <u>surface</u>. This means that Joyce

- Ⓐ had just heard happy news.
- Ⓑ appeared to be happy.
- Ⓒ was certainly very happy.
- Ⓓ had a cheerful personality.

12. Who would most need a <u>ramp</u>?

- Ⓐ someone who has a broken arm
- Ⓑ someone who uses a wheelchair
- Ⓒ someone who is looking for a job
- Ⓓ someone who is cooking dinner

13. What is on an apple's <u>surface</u>?

- Ⓐ its seeds
- Ⓑ its skin
- Ⓒ its juice
- Ⓓ its core

14. What do workers get from a <u>quarry</u>?

- Ⓐ milk
- Ⓑ crops
- Ⓒ stone
- Ⓓ cloth

15. Which is a <u>portion</u> of one dollar?

- Ⓐ 25¢
- Ⓑ 100¢
- Ⓒ $4.00
- Ⓓ $1.00

16. What is the <u>location</u> of the Eiffel Tower?

- Ⓐ lawns, trees, and flowers
- Ⓑ a famous landmark
- Ⓒ 1,063 feet
- Ⓓ Paris, France

17. What might someone say to an <u>intruder</u>?

- Ⓐ "Welcome!"
- Ⓑ "Get out!"
- Ⓒ "Thank you for delivering this package."
- Ⓓ "Goodbye. It was nice to see you again."

18. Which of these describes an <u>intrusion</u>?

    Ⓐ   a family member arriving at someone's birthday party

    Ⓑ   a stranger entering someone's home

    Ⓒ   a worker arriving for work in the morning

    Ⓓ   an important phone call

19. Which is an <u>interior</u> space?

    Ⓐ   a backyard

    Ⓑ   a driveway

    Ⓒ   a roof

    Ⓓ   a living room

20. Which of these has <u>entries</u>?

    Ⓐ   a watermelon

    Ⓑ   a diary

    Ⓒ   a chair

    Ⓓ   a jellyfish

21. Who are Pablo Picasso's <u>descendants</u>?

    Ⓐ   the people in his paintings

    Ⓑ   his friends

    Ⓒ   his parents

    Ⓓ   his great-grandchildren

22. How long is a <u>century</u>?

    Ⓐ   one year

    Ⓑ   ten years

    Ⓒ   one hundred years

    Ⓓ   one thousand years

For items 23–26, find the word that means about the SAME as the underlined word. Then fill in the circle next to your answer.

23. <u>locate</u>

    Ⓐ   grab

    Ⓑ   find

    Ⓒ   glimpse

    Ⓓ   examine

24. <u>passage</u>

      Ⓐ   rug

      Ⓑ   window

      Ⓒ   room

      Ⓓ   hallway

25. <u>portion</u>

      Ⓐ   soup

      Ⓑ   spoon

      Ⓒ   serving

      Ⓓ   drink

26. <u>spacious</u>

      Ⓐ   heavy

      Ⓑ   short

      Ⓒ   round

      Ⓓ   roomy

For items 27–30, find the word that means the OPPOSITE of the underlined word. Then fill in the circle next to your answer.

27. <u>descend</u>

      Ⓐ   roll

      Ⓑ   shrink

      Ⓒ   rise

      Ⓓ   widen

28. <u>interior</u>

      Ⓐ   outside

      Ⓑ   top

      Ⓒ   bottom

      Ⓓ   left side

29. <u>precious</u>

      Ⓐ   dirty

      Ⓑ   worthless

      Ⓒ   rough

      Ⓓ   ugly

30. <u>surface</u>

    Ⓐ   circle

    Ⓑ   dive

    Ⓒ   zigzag

    Ⓓ   wander

Book 4, Lesson 9 Test

Choose the BEST way to complete each sentence or answer each question. Then fill in the circle next to your answer.

1. What is an <u>advantage</u>?

   Ⓐ   something useless

   Ⓑ   something helpful

   Ⓒ   something don't like to do

   Ⓓ   something you like to do

2. A <u>hamlet</u> is a

   Ⓐ   kind of store.

   Ⓑ   kind of horse and wagon.

   Ⓒ   small piece of ham.

   Ⓓ   small village.

3. To be <u>parched</u> is to be

   Ⓐ   very late.

   Ⓑ   very old.

   Ⓒ   very thirsty.

   Ⓓ   very hungry.

4. A <u>typical</u> breakfast food is

   Ⓐ   cereal.

   Ⓑ   hamburgers and hot dogs.

   Ⓒ   salad.

   Ⓓ   apple pie.

5. A <u>founder</u> of a store is the person who

   Ⓐ   keeps it going.

   Ⓑ   gets it started.

   Ⓒ   writes the ads.

   Ⓓ   sells to people who shop in the store.

6. Maleek <u>took advantage of</u> the work I did for him by

Ⓐ paying me more than he said he would.

Ⓑ paying me less than he said he would.

Ⓒ telling me what a great job I had done.

Ⓓ telling me what a poor job I had done.

7. Carmen was <u>astonished</u> by the sight of

Ⓐ a bird in her back yard.

Ⓑ a child riding a bike.

Ⓒ a man walking his dog.

Ⓓ a deer crossing a busy street.

8. In the <u>distance</u> Miranda could see

Ⓐ the burrow of a woodchuck.

Ⓑ an ant at her feet.

Ⓒ a rainbow.

Ⓓ a crack in the sidewalk.

9. Which means the OPPOSITE of a <u>host</u> of people?

Ⓐ a small number of people

Ⓑ all the people in town

Ⓒ one hundred people

Ⓓ a lot of people

10. To <u>torment</u> is to cause

Ⓐ pain.

Ⓑ joy.

Ⓒ fear.

Ⓓ confusion.

11. Which means the OPPOSITE of <u>scarce</u>?

Ⓐ cozy

Ⓑ plentiful

Ⓒ delicious

Ⓓ comfortable

12. When might you have a <u>misgiving</u>?

    Ⓐ   when the weekend arrives.

    Ⓑ   when you are looking forward to having a friend come over.

    Ⓒ   after a big dinner.

    Ⓓ   when you are worried about something that may happen.

13. What is the <u>prospect</u> of finding a shoe store open at 6 AM?

    Ⓐ   poor

    Ⓑ   good

    Ⓒ   fair

    Ⓓ   excellent

14. Which of these describes a <u>sole</u> traveler on a train?

    Ⓐ   two people going to Florida

    Ⓑ   a mother and child walking to the dining car

    Ⓒ   a man reading a newspaper by the window

    Ⓓ   three people talking

15. Where is the <u>sole</u> of a shoe?

    Ⓐ   on the top

    Ⓑ   on the bottom

    Ⓒ   on the side

    Ⓓ   under the laces

16. Which of these is a <u>prospector</u>?

    Ⓐ   a fortuneteller

    Ⓑ   a job seeker

    Ⓒ   an explorer

    Ⓓ   a scientist

17. When there is a <u>scarcity</u> of food,

    Ⓐ   there is more than enough food for everyone.

    Ⓑ   there is not enough food.

    Ⓒ   there will be a good amount of food in a month or so.

    Ⓓ   there is just enough food for the number of people there.

18. If you <u>confirm</u> a meeting with your teacher,

    Ⓐ   you set up the meeting.

    Ⓑ   you meet a day before you had planned.

    Ⓒ   you change the day of the meeting to next week.

    Ⓓ   you check to make sure of the day and time you will meet.

19. If the city council votes to <u>confirm</u> the town manager,

    Ⓐ   it approves the manager's job.

    Ⓑ   it votes down the manager's job.

    Ⓒ   it puts off voting on the manager's job.

    Ⓓ   it calls for a revote for the manager's job.

20. Which of these describes a ship that is <u>foundering</u>?

    Ⓐ   a ship that is tossing in the waves

    Ⓑ   a ship that is sailing smoothly along

    Ⓒ   a ship that is sinking

    Ⓓ   a ship that is moving very slowly

21. A <u>host</u> at a restaurant

    Ⓐ   greets you and shows you to your table.

    Ⓑ   sets the table.

    Ⓒ   cooks your food.

    Ⓓ   washes your dishes.

22. <u>Sole</u> is a type of

    Ⓐ   dog.

    Ⓑ   cat.

    Ⓒ   fish.

    Ⓓ   bird.

For items 23–27, find the word that means about the SAME as the underlined word. Then fill in the circle next to your answer.

23. <u>shrewd</u>

    Ⓐ   vain

    Ⓑ   clever

    Ⓒ   abrupt

    Ⓓ   loud

24. <u>parch</u>

  Ⓐ make wet

  Ⓑ replace

  Ⓒ make dry

  Ⓓ increase

25. <u>distant</u>

  Ⓐ nearby

  Ⓑ loud

  Ⓒ lacking

  Ⓓ far away

26. <u>astonishment</u>

  Ⓐ curiosity

  Ⓑ contentment

  Ⓒ relaxation

  Ⓓ amazement

27. <u>torment</u>

  Ⓐ deep suffering

  Ⓑ hibernation

  Ⓒ bliss

  Ⓓ great joy

Name: _____ Date: _____

Book 4, Lesson 10 Test

Choose the BEST way to complete each sentence or answer each question. Then fill in the circle next to your answer.

1. To <u>regain</u> your strength is to

   Ⓐ brag about it.

   Ⓑ get it back.

   Ⓒ lift a heavy object.

   Ⓓ grow weaker.

2. An <u>orphan</u> has no

   Ⓐ place to live.

   Ⓑ children.

   Ⓒ brothers and sisters.

   Ⓓ parents.

3. A person's <u>livelihood</u> is

   Ⓐ that person's favorite pastime.

   Ⓑ how that person supports himself.

   Ⓒ that person's family.

   Ⓓ how that person makes friends.

4. "What <u>ails</u> you?" means the same as

   Ⓐ "What is the matter?"

   Ⓑ "How are you?"

   Ⓒ "Where are you going?"

   Ⓓ "How is it going?"

5. To <u>banish</u> sorrow is to

   Ⓐ feel miserable.

   Ⓑ get rid of it completely.

   Ⓒ cry.

   Ⓓ feel a little sad.

6. To <u>communicate</u> important news is to

   Ⓐ   tell it to someone.

   Ⓑ   learn about it.

   Ⓒ   think about it.

   Ⓓ   listen to a radio news program.

7. People most often <u>deliberate</u> about

   Ⓐ   brushing their teeth.

   Ⓑ   important decisions.

   Ⓒ   pieces of junk mail.

   Ⓓ   jokes.

8. To <u>desire</u> new clothes is to

   Ⓐ   buy some.

   Ⓑ   decide not to buy any.

   Ⓒ   want some very much.

   Ⓓ   forget to buy them.

9. The <u>depth</u> of a desk drawer is

   Ⓐ   how handy it is.

   Ⓑ   what color it is.

   Ⓒ   how deep it is.

   Ⓓ   how heavy it is.

10. When is a dog most likely to <u>cower</u>?

   Ⓐ   when it is sleepy

   Ⓑ   when it is hungry

   Ⓒ   when it is excited about going for a walk

   Ⓓ   when someone shouts angrily at it

11. When is someone most likely to <u>console</u> a child?

   Ⓐ   when the child is asleep

   Ⓑ   when the child is sad

   Ⓒ   when the child is laughing

   Ⓓ   when the child is eating

12. Which is an example of <u>communication</u>?

  Ⓐ taking a walk

  Ⓑ talking on the phone

  Ⓒ daydreaming

  Ⓓ cooking dinner

13. Which of these is a <u>misfortune</u>?

  Ⓐ a steep cliff

  Ⓑ a car accident

  Ⓒ a national holiday

  Ⓓ a long weekend

14. Which of these is a cold <u>symptom</u>?

  Ⓐ cold weather

  Ⓑ drinking lots of juice

  Ⓒ a sore throat

  Ⓓ medicine

For items 15–22, find the word that means about the SAME as the underlined word. Then fill in the circle next to your answer.

15. <u>ailment</u>

  Ⓐ argument

  Ⓑ sorrow

  Ⓒ color

  Ⓓ illness

16. <u>consolation</u>

  Ⓐ advice

  Ⓑ comfort

  Ⓒ joy

  Ⓓ payment

17. <u>desire</u>

  Ⓐ instruction

  Ⓑ wish

  Ⓒ command

  Ⓓ intention

18. <u>desirable</u>

    Ⓐ warm

    Ⓑ soft

    Ⓒ pleasing

    Ⓓ shiny

19. <u>misfortune</u>

    Ⓐ trouble

    Ⓑ misbehavior

    Ⓒ argument

    Ⓓ discomfort

20. <u>precipice</u>

    Ⓐ cliff

    Ⓑ valley

    Ⓒ ditch

    Ⓓ hill

21. <u>precipitous</u>

    Ⓐ icy

    Ⓑ rocky

    Ⓒ steep

    Ⓓ snowy

22. <u>slay</u>

    Ⓐ wound

    Ⓑ harm

    Ⓒ injure

    Ⓓ kill

For items 23–28, find the word that means the OPPOSITE of the underlined word. Then fill in the circle next to your answer.

23. <u>ailing</u>

    Ⓐ busy

    Ⓑ pretty

    Ⓒ funny

    Ⓓ healthy

24. <u>banish</u>

    Ⓐ   invite

    Ⓑ   aid

    Ⓒ   heal

    Ⓓ   love

25. <u>communicative</u>

    Ⓐ   sorrowful

    Ⓑ   angry

    Ⓒ   silent

    Ⓓ   irritable

26. <u>depths</u>

    Ⓐ   surface

    Ⓑ   width

    Ⓒ   length

    Ⓓ   weight

27. <u>deliberate</u>

    Ⓐ   destructive

    Ⓑ   warlike

    Ⓒ   fearful

    Ⓓ   hasty

28. <u>precipitous</u>

    Ⓐ   generous

    Ⓑ   satisfying

    Ⓒ   comforting

    Ⓓ   deliberate

Name: _____ Date: _____

Book 4, Midterm Test 1 (Lessons 1–10)

Read the passage. Choose the BEST answer for each sentence or question about an underlined word. Then fill in the circle next to your answer.

NADIA COMANECI'S PERFECT TENS

It was 1976 in Montreal, Canada. Nadia Comaneci, a fourteen-year-old gymnast, was <u>representing</u> Romania at the Olympic Games. The strong, <u>graceful</u> teenager with the perky ponytail wasn't even five feet tall. She weighed only eighty-six pounds. Yet Nadia <u>achieved</u> a record matched by no other Olympian.

On the first day of the gymnastics competition, Comaneci showed off her skill on the uneven <u>parallel</u> bars. She seemed to have <u>limbs</u> of steel. Her muscular yet <u>flexible</u> arms and legs let her swing around the bars as effortlessly as a bird swooping in flight. At the end of her routine, she <u>descended</u> to the floor mat in a flawless landing. Her feet were together and her arms were beautifully extended. The judges confirmed Nadia's talent by awarding her the highest score possible—a perfect ten. The audience was <u>astounded</u> and <u>applauded</u> wildly when they saw her score.

But this was just the beginning. Nadia Comaneci continued to <u>astonish</u> judges, spectators, and television viewers around the globe. She earned six more perfect scores. She was awarded three Olympic gold medals: in the uneven bars, the balance beam, and the all-around competition.

Of course, Nadia Comaneci did not become such a spectacular athlete without practice. It took her many years to <u>prepare</u> for the Olympic Games. When she was only six years old, the famous gymnastics coach Bela Karolyi spied her playing on a playground in Onesti, Romania. Apparently Nadia's talent was clear even then. Karolyi asked her family's permission to take the little girl to his classes. Soon he began training her for competition. Besides grace, strength, and flexibility, little Nadia had a strong <u>desire</u> to compete and win. At the Montreal Olympics, her many years of hard work finally paid off.

1. Read this sentence from the story.

Nadia Comaneci, a fourteen-year-old gymnast, was <u>representing</u> Romania at the Olympic Games.
This sentence means that Nadia was

    Ⓐ   running for office in the Romanian government.

    Ⓑ   an athlete on the Romanian Olympic team.

    Ⓒ   a coach for the Romanian Olympic team.

    Ⓓ   fighting the Romanian government.

2. In this passage, <u>graceful</u> means

    Ⓐ   polite.

    Ⓑ   generous.

    Ⓒ   having beautiful movements.

    Ⓓ   having a strong competitive spirit.

3. Read this sentence from the story.

Yet Nadia <u>achieved</u> a record matched by no other Olympian.
In this sentence, <u>achieved</u> means

    Ⓐ   reached.

    Ⓑ   barely missed.

    Ⓒ   hoped for.

    Ⓓ   wrote down.

4. Read this sentence from the story.

On the first day of the gymnastics competition, Comaneci showed off her skill on the uneven <u>parallel</u> bars.
What does <u>parallel</u> mean?

    Ⓐ   uneven

    Ⓑ   crossed

    Ⓒ   lying in opposite directions and the same distance apart

    Ⓓ   lying in the same direction and the same distance apart

5. Read this sentence from the story.

She seemed to have <u>limbs</u> of steel.
What does this sentence mean?

    Ⓐ   Nadia's hands were very strong.

    Ⓑ   Nadia's arms and legs were very strong.

    Ⓒ   Nadia's garden had trees with strong, thick branches.

    Ⓓ   Nadia's desire to win was very strong.

6. Read this sentence from the story.

Her muscular yet <u>flexible</u> arms and legs let her swing around the bars as effortlessly as a bird swooping in flight.

In this sentence, <u>flexible</u> means

    Ⓐ   able to lift heavy weights.

    Ⓑ   able to bend easily.

    Ⓒ   able to fly like a bird.

    Ⓓ   able to adjust to new situations.

7. What does <u>descended</u> mean in this passage?

    Ⓐ   to run

    Ⓑ   to fly

    Ⓒ   to move down

    Ⓓ   to move sideways

8. In this passage, "the audience was <u>astounded</u>" means they

    Ⓐ   were amazed by her talent.

    Ⓑ   did not think she had talent.

    Ⓒ   thought her landing was strong.

    Ⓓ   wanted her to repeat her routine.

9. In this passage, "the audience <u>applauded</u>" means

    Ⓐ   the audience laughed.

    Ⓑ   the audience clapped their hands.

    Ⓒ   the audience protested.

    Ⓓ   the audience watched very carefully.

10. Read this sentence from the story.

Nadia Comaneci continued to <u>astonish</u> judges, spectators, and television viewers around the globe.

Which word means about the same as <u>astonish</u>?

    Ⓐ   charm

    Ⓑ   persuade

    Ⓒ   amaze

    Ⓓ   fool

11. Read these sentences from the story.

Of course, Nadia Comaneci did not become such a spectacular athlete without practice. It took her many years to <u>prepare</u> for the Olympic Games.

Which means about the same as <u>prepare</u>?

    Ⓐ   try out

    Ⓑ   fight

    Ⓒ   compete

    Ⓓ   get ready

12. In this passage, <u>desire</u> means about the same as

    Ⓐ   ability.

    Ⓑ   wish.

    Ⓒ   reason.

    Ⓓ   curiosity.

Book 4, Midterm Test 2 (Lessons 1–10)

Read the passage. Choose the BEST answer for each sentence or question about an underlined word. Then fill in the circle next to your answer.

PRAIRIE DOGS

Prairie dogs are not really dogs. They are short-tailed squirrels that live in underground <u>burrows</u>. Their habitat is the North American prairie. Prairie dogs got their name from the way they <u>communicate</u> with one another in barks and yips. The animals reminded French explorers of their pets back home, and the explorers named them *petits chiens*, or "little dogs."

Prairie dogs live in large colonies. They watch out for one another by posting sentries. These are prairie dogs that sit upright atop a mound of earth to spot predators. From this little hill the sentry can spot <u>approaching</u> predators before they get too close. The sentries feel <u>uneasy</u> if they cannot see all around them, so prairie dogs keep the grass near their homes clipped short.

If a sentry spots an <u>intruder</u>, it warns the community with a special warning bark. All prairie dogs in the open <u>scurry</u> underground to safety. Sometimes a predator will follow prairie dogs underground, but the prairie dogs have a solution. They respond by quickly plugging up their tunnels with dirt. While the predator is digging itself out, the prairie dogs have a chance to escape.

When danger has passed, prairie dogs give an "all clear" signal. Scientists who <u>observe</u> prairie dogs have named this the "jump-yip" sign. This behavior can be <u>entertaining</u> to watch. Yipping excitedly, the prairie dog flips its front legs into the air and jumps right off its hind legs. It looks like an enthusiastic sports fan doing "the wave" in a stadium.

Prairie dog communities are <u>organized</u> into families, larger groups called wards, and even larger ones called towns or colonies. In the past, some prairie dog towns were huge. A single town in Texas <u>exceeded</u> 20,000 square miles!

Today, numbers of prairie dogs are dropping. Some wildlife groups want prairie dogs to be protected by law. Prairie dogs are a "keystone" species. This means that their survival <u>affects</u> many other animals and plants. One prairie dog predator, the black-footed ferret, came dangerously close to dying out. Wildlife workers are struggling to save this rare animal, a cousin of the weasel. Predators such as coyotes, rattlesnakes, and eagles also depend on prairie dogs as part of their diet. Burrowing owls, newts, and many other creatures find shelter in prairie dog tunnels. Prairie dogs' grass-clipping behavior <u>benefits</u> grazing animals such as cattle, antelopes, and American bison. When prairie dogs clip the grass, it causes higher-quality grass to grow.

1. In this passage, <u>burrows</u> means

   Ⓐ   tunnels used as homes.

   Ⓑ   caves used as homes.

   Ⓒ   hollow trees used as homes.

   Ⓓ   searches through.

2. In this passage, <u>communicate</u> means

   Ⓐ   to watch for predators.

   Ⓑ   to change other animals' lives.

   Ⓒ   to exchange information.

   Ⓓ   to search for food.

3. In this passage, "an <u>approaching</u> predator" means

   Ⓐ   a dangerous predator.

   Ⓑ   a fierce predator.

   Ⓒ   a predator that is coming closer.

   Ⓓ   a predator that lives underground.

4. Why do prairie dogs feel <u>uneasy</u> if they cannot see all around them?

   Ⓐ   because they cannot find water

   Ⓑ   because they cannot find food

   Ⓒ   because they cannot see predators coming

   Ⓓ   because a beautiful view comforts them

5. The <u>intruder</u> mentioned in this passage is

   Ⓐ   an unwelcome party guest.

   Ⓑ   a predator or person coming toward a prairie dog burrow.

   Ⓒ   a scientist who is observing a prairie dog town.

   Ⓓ   someone who does not have permission to be in a wildlife park.

6. When an animal <u>scurries</u>, it

   Ⓐ   makes yipping sounds.

   Ⓑ   barks like a dog.

   Ⓒ   digs an underground tunnel.

   Ⓓ   moves with rapid little steps.

7. To <u>observe</u> prairie dogs is to

    Ⓐ   protect them.

    Ⓑ   feed them.

    Ⓒ   amuse them.

    Ⓓ   watch them.

8. In this passage, <u>entertaining</u> means

    Ⓐ   amusing.

    Ⓑ   performing.

    Ⓒ   educational.

    Ⓓ   exhausting.

9. In this passage, <u>organized</u> means

    Ⓐ   started.

    Ⓑ   grouped.

    Ⓒ   tidied up.

    Ⓓ   scheduled.

10. This passage states that "one prairie dog town <u>exceeded</u> 20,000 square miles." How big could that town have been?

    Ⓐ   500 square miles

    Ⓑ   10,000 square miles

    Ⓒ   19,000 square miles

    Ⓓ   25,000 square miles

11. Read these sentences from the passage.

Prairie dogs are a "keystone" species. This means that their survival <u>affects</u> many other animals and plants.

This means that the prairie dogs' survival

    Ⓐ   can create other animals and plants

    Ⓑ   can feed other animals and plants

    Ⓒ   can cause changes to other animals and plants

    Ⓓ   has nothing to do with other animals and plants

12. Read this sentence from the passage.

Prairie dogs' grass-clipping behavior <u>benefits</u> grazing animals such as cattle, antelopes, and American bison.

In this sentence, what does <u>benefits</u> mean?

    Ⓐ   receives help

    Ⓑ   helps

    Ⓒ   a helpful act

    Ⓓ   to feel grateful

Name: _____ Date: _____

Book 4, Lesson 11 Test

Choose the BEST way to complete each sentence or answer each question. Then fill in the circle next to your answer.

1. An <u>annual</u> holiday comes

   Ⓐ   twice a year.

   Ⓑ   once a month.

   Ⓒ   on a weekend.

   Ⓓ   once a year.

2. To <u>blend</u> butter, eggs, and sugar is to

   Ⓐ   bake them.

   Ⓑ   mix them together.

   Ⓒ   measure them.

   Ⓓ   keep them refrigerated.

3. When two singers' voices <u>blend</u> well, they

   Ⓐ   sound exactly the same.

   Ⓑ   sing low notes well.

   Ⓒ   sing high notes well.

   Ⓓ   go together well.

4. To <u>bore</u> a hole is to

   Ⓐ   dig one with a shovel.

   Ⓑ   burrow into the ground.

   Ⓒ   make one by drilling.

   Ⓓ   make one by sawing.

5. To <u>bore</u> someone is to

   Ⓐ   hire that person to do a job.

   Ⓑ   tell that person a story.

   Ⓒ   help that person.

   Ⓓ   tire that person by being dull.

6. A <u>considerable</u> amount of money is

    Ⓐ   not enough.

    Ⓑ   the amount someone has saved.

    Ⓒ   a large amount.

    Ⓓ   just enough.

7. <u>Crude</u> oil

    Ⓐ   powers cars.

    Ⓑ   has not been refined.

    Ⓒ   is a salad dressing ingredient.

    Ⓓ   powers airplanes.

8. A <u>crude</u> drawing is

    Ⓐ   colorful.

    Ⓑ   carefully made.

    Ⓒ   a charcoal drawing.

    Ⓓ   roughly made.

9. A price <u>increase</u> is the OPPOSITE of

    Ⓐ   a price drop.

    Ⓑ   a moderate price.

    Ⓒ   a fair price.

    Ⓓ   a ridiculous price.

10. A peach tree's <u>yield</u> is

    Ⓐ   the farmer who planted it.

    Ⓑ   the amount of fruit it produces.

    Ⓒ   its height.

    Ⓓ   its flowers.

11. To <u>vary</u> the way you dress is to

    Ⓐ   plan what you will wear.

    Ⓑ   take good care of your clothes.

    Ⓒ   wear different outfits.

    Ⓓ   dress sloppily.

12. A <u>visual</u> clue can be

   Ⓐ   heard.

   Ⓑ   seen.

   Ⓒ   smelled.

   Ⓓ   tasted.

13. A <u>vision</u> of the future is

   Ⓐ   a great grandchild.

   Ⓑ   how someone imagines the future.

   Ⓒ   a time machine.

   Ⓓ   someone who predicts the future.

14. When I was sick, my appetite <u>evaporated</u>. In this sentence, <u>evaporated</u> means

   Ⓐ   grew stronger.

   Ⓑ   was hard to satisfy.

   Ⓒ   grew simpler.

   Ⓓ   disappeared.

15. Which provides <u>nourishment</u> for honeybees?

   Ⓐ   rain

   Ⓑ   smoke

   Ⓒ   stingers

   Ⓓ   honey

16. How often will a high school print its <u>annual</u>?

   Ⓐ   once a month

   Ⓑ   every six months

   Ⓒ   once a year

   Ⓓ   every two years

17. What happens to water when it <u>evaporates</u>?

   Ⓐ   It freezes.

   Ⓑ   It melts.

   Ⓒ   It turns to vapor.

   Ⓓ   It turns to mud.

18. Maria and her mother planted <u>annuals</u> in their garden. How long will those plants live?

    Ⓐ   one year

    Ⓑ   six months

    Ⓒ   three months

    Ⓓ   many years

19. Which of these people is most likely a <u>bore</u>?

    Ⓐ   Erik, who has an interesting family

    Ⓑ   Fiona, who tells funny jokes

    Ⓒ   Geeta, who tells dull stories

    Ⓓ   Harold, who is a fascinating speaker

20. Which of these <u>yields</u> milk?

    Ⓐ   a drinking glass

    Ⓑ   a baby

    Ⓒ   butter

    Ⓓ   a cow

For items 21–28, find the word that means about the SAME as the underlined word. Then fill in the circle next to your answer.

21. <u>yield</u>

    Ⓐ   wave

    Ⓑ   surrender

    Ⓒ   aid

    Ⓓ   greet

22. <u>boring</u>

    Ⓐ   relaxing

    Ⓑ   comforting

    Ⓒ   dull

    Ⓓ   exhausting

23. <u>nourish</u>

    Ⓐ   desire

    Ⓑ   support

    Ⓒ   resent

    Ⓓ   groom

24. <u>vision</u>

    Ⓐ   eyesight

    Ⓑ   hearing

    Ⓒ   smell

    Ⓓ   taste

25. <u>foliage</u>

    Ⓐ   roots

    Ⓑ   leaves

    Ⓒ   limbs

    Ⓓ   branches

26. <u>gash</u>

    Ⓐ   scrape

    Ⓑ   burn

    Ⓒ   cut

    Ⓓ   fracture

27. <u>hue</u>

    Ⓐ   color

    Ⓑ   texture

    Ⓒ   pattern

    Ⓓ   scent

28. <u>blend</u>

    Ⓐ   substance

    Ⓑ   paste

    Ⓒ   liquid

    Ⓓ   mixture

For items 29–33, find the word that means the OPPOSITE of the underlined word. Then fill in the circle next to your answer.

29. <u>boredom</u>

    Ⓐ   sorrow

    Ⓑ   relaxation

    Ⓒ   exhaustion

    Ⓓ   interest

30. <u>artificial</u>

    Ⓐ   intelligent

    Ⓑ   natural

    Ⓒ   gentle

    Ⓓ   generous

31. <u>crude</u>

    Ⓐ   cautious

    Ⓑ   hard-working

    Ⓒ   rude

    Ⓓ   well-mannered

32. <u>increase</u>

    Ⓐ   alter

    Ⓑ   stretch

    Ⓒ   widen

    Ⓓ   reduce

33. <u>variation</u>

    Ⓐ   similarity

    Ⓑ   expansion

    Ⓒ   increase

    Ⓓ   reduction

Copyright protected by Education Publishing Service Reproducing any part of this workbook is prohibited by law.

Book 4, Lesson 12 Test

Choose the BEST way to complete each sentence or answer each question. Then fill in the circle next to your answer.

1. A <u>caress</u> is a

   Ⓐ   handshake.

   Ⓑ   loving touch.

   Ⓒ   powerful shove.

   Ⓓ   sudden yank.

2. A <u>clutch</u> is part of a

   Ⓐ   dog.

   Ⓑ   car.

   Ⓒ   tree.

   Ⓓ   shirt.

3. To <u>coax</u> is to

   Ⓐ   command.

   Ⓑ   interrupt.

   Ⓒ   persuade gently.

   Ⓓ   ask slyly.

4. Someone who is <u>furious</u> is very

   Ⓐ   sad.

   Ⓑ   angry.

   Ⓒ   curious.

   Ⓓ   bored.

5. To move at a <u>furious</u> pace is to go

   Ⓐ   in a circle.

   Ⓑ   away.

   Ⓒ   back and forth.

   Ⓓ   very fast.

6. A hurricane's <u>fury</u> is

    Ⓐ   its uncontrollable force.

    Ⓑ   the amount of rain it brings.

    Ⓒ   the time when it is expected to arrive.

    Ⓓ   one of its victims.

7. Sending a birthday card to your friend is a loving

    Ⓐ   <u>request</u>.

    Ⓑ   <u>caress</u>.

    Ⓒ   <u>gesture</u>.

    Ⓓ   <u>preference</u>.

8. Someone who <u>mopes</u> is feeling

    Ⓐ   gloomy.

    Ⓑ   nervous.

    Ⓒ   excited.

    Ⓓ   relieved.

9. A <u>preference</u> is someone's

    Ⓐ   name.

    Ⓑ   address.

    Ⓒ   first choice.

    Ⓓ   personality trait.

10. To <u>recover</u> is to

    Ⓐ   buy something new.

    Ⓑ   get well again.

    Ⓒ   get a new job.

    Ⓓ   move to a new home.

11. To <u>prefer</u> green is to

    Ⓐ   paint with it.

    Ⓑ   dye a shirt green.

    Ⓒ   create it by mixing yellow and blue.

    Ⓓ   like it better than other colors.

12. A <u>gesture</u> is a movement of the

    Ⓐ   foot or leg.

    Ⓑ   eyes.

    Ⓒ   hand or arm.

    Ⓓ   mouth.

13. A <u>recovery</u> period is a time when someone is

    Ⓐ   returning to normal after being sick.

    Ⓑ   studying for an important test.

    Ⓒ   packing to move to a new home.

    Ⓓ   training for an athletic event.

14. Which of the following is a <u>recovery</u>?

    Ⓐ   buying a new computer.

    Ⓑ   repairing a broken computer.

    Ⓒ   reporting a lost wallet.

    Ⓓ   getting a lost wallet back.

15. To <u>replace</u> a book on a bookshelf is to

    Ⓐ   dust it off.

    Ⓑ   put it back.

    Ⓒ   pick it up.

    Ⓓ   choose to read it.

16. To <u>request</u> a book from the library is to

    Ⓐ   read it.

    Ⓑ   write a report about it.

    Ⓒ   return it late.

    Ⓓ   ask for it.

17. Iliana will <u>replace</u> Tyler in the school play. What does <u>replace</u> mean in this sentence?

    Ⓐ   to play the role of

    Ⓑ   to cooperate with

    Ⓒ   to take the place of

    Ⓓ   to argue with

18. Nadia and Malcolm go to <u>separate</u> schools. This means that they

    Ⓐ   go to good schools.

    Ⓑ   go to school in a small town.

    Ⓒ   go to two different schools.

    Ⓓ   go to a city school.

19. Which describes a <u>request</u>?

    Ⓐ   a popular band's concert

    Ⓑ   a song that is on a popular band's CD

    Ⓒ   a movie about a popular band

    Ⓓ   a song that someone asks a radio station to play

20. Which is a friendly dog most likely to <u>shun</u>?

    Ⓐ   a smaller friendly dog

    Ⓑ   the dog's owner

    Ⓒ   a child

    Ⓓ   a skunk

21. Which is a <u>gesture</u>?

    Ⓐ   waving goodbye

    Ⓑ   lying down

    Ⓒ   running in circles

    Ⓓ   sitting down

22. The Ramirez family had a <u>blissful</u> celebration. What kind of celebration did they have?

    Ⓐ   a large celebration

    Ⓑ   a joyful celebration

    Ⓒ   a birthday celebration

    Ⓓ   a celebration with a lot of food

For items 23–27, find the word that means about the SAME as the underlined word. Then fill in the circle next to your answer.

23. <u>replacement</u>

    Ⓐ   substitute

    Ⓑ   principal

    Ⓒ   teacher

    Ⓓ   student

24. <u>fury</u>

   Ⓐ distrust

   Ⓑ sorrow

   Ⓒ anger

   Ⓓ boredom

25. <u>clutch</u>

   Ⓐ yank

   Ⓑ caress

   Ⓒ touch

   Ⓓ grasp

26. <u>ability</u>

   Ⓐ skill

   Ⓑ fear

   Ⓒ choice

   Ⓓ sadness

27. <u>caress</u>

   Ⓐ push

   Ⓑ twirl

   Ⓒ touch

   Ⓓ strike

For items 28–31, find the word that means the OPPOSITE of the underlined word. Then fill in the circle next to your answer.

28. <u>amiable</u>

   Ⓐ silly

   Ⓑ crafty

   Ⓒ envious

   Ⓓ unfriendly

29. <u>bliss</u>

   Ⓐ boredom

   Ⓑ exhaustion

   Ⓒ sorrow

   Ⓓ malice

30. <u>recovered</u>

   Ⓐ stained

   Ⓑ torn

   Ⓒ wrinkled

   Ⓓ lost

31. <u>separate</u>

   Ⓐ join

   Ⓑ sprinkle

   Ⓒ pour

   Ⓓ distribute

Book 4, Lesson 13 Test

Choose the BEST way to complete each sentence or answer each question. Then fill in the circle next to your answer.

1. A <u>fanatic</u> is someone who

   Ⓐ is from a large family.

   Ⓑ is extremely enthusiastic about his or her beliefs.

   Ⓒ has creative ideas.

   Ⓓ has his or her own business.

2. To make an <u>impact</u> on someone is to

   Ⓐ make an impression on that person.

   Ⓑ make a deal with that person.

   Ⓒ make friends with that person.

   Ⓓ treat that person as your guest.

3. Julia is a <u>fanatic</u> comic book collector. This means that she

   Ⓐ has a very small comic book collection.

   Ⓑ is extremely interested in collecting comic books.

   Ⓒ collects only valuable comic books.

   Ⓓ is just beginning to collect comic books.

4. To <u>isolate</u> someone is to

   Ⓐ teach that person a lesson.

   Ⓑ celebrate with that person.

   Ⓒ speak angrily to that person.

   Ⓓ separate that person from others.

5. Someone who <u>occupies</u> an apartment

   Ⓐ cleans the apartment.

   Ⓑ delivers mail to the apartment.

   Ⓒ lives in the apartment.

   Ⓓ owns the apartment building.

6. To protest the new land fill, we planned to <u>occupy</u> the lawn of city hall. What does <u>occupy</u> mean in this sentence?

    Ⓐ   take care of

    Ⓑ   take over

    Ⓒ   surround

    Ⓓ   decorate

7. To <u>rout</u> your opponents is to

    Ⓐ   fear them.

    Ⓑ   defeat them.

    Ⓒ   respect their athletic skills.

    Ⓓ   play almost as well as they do.

8. A <u>tragedy</u> is an event that causes

    Ⓐ   great suffering.

    Ⓑ   a car accident.

    Ⓒ   an earthquake.

    Ⓓ   a flood.

9. To <u>suspect</u> someone is to

    Ⓐ   get to know that person.

    Ⓑ   find that person fascinating.

    Ⓒ   worry about that person.

    Ⓓ   think that person is guilty.

10. A <u>suspect</u> is someone

    Ⓐ   who works as a police officer.

    Ⓑ   who works as a detective.

    Ⓒ   whom others think is guilty.

    Ⓓ   who goes to jail for committing a crime.

11. What is <u>terror</u>?

    Ⓐ   great fear

    Ⓑ   mild anger

    Ⓒ   great joy

    Ⓓ   worry

12. That movie <u>terrified</u> Jonah. How did it make Jonah feel?

- Ⓐ bored
- Ⓑ confused
- Ⓒ extremely angry
- Ⓓ very scared

13. A <u>tragedy</u> is a play that ends

- Ⓐ after two acts.
- Ⓑ sadly.
- Ⓒ happily.
- Ⓓ suddenly.

14. We <u>occupied</u> our time by playing dominoes. What does <u>occupied</u> mean in this sentence?

- Ⓐ we filled up time
- Ⓑ we wasted time
- Ⓒ we enjoyed ourselves
- Ⓓ we played all day

15. Who or what might <u>invade</u> a country?

- Ⓐ an enemy army
- Ⓑ that country's own army
- Ⓒ a group of tourists
- Ⓓ a river

16. Which was a <u>tragic</u> event?

- Ⓐ the first Moon landing on July 20, 1969
- Ⓑ the sinking of the Titanic on April 15, 1912
- Ⓒ the Winter Olympic Games in 2002
- Ⓓ the beginning of a new millennium on January 1, 2000

17. When might you wish for <u>isolation</u>?

- Ⓐ when you are hungry
- Ⓑ when you need advice
- Ⓒ when you want to be by yourself
- Ⓓ when you feel like going to a party

18. Who is most likely to feel <u>isolated</u>?

    Ⓐ   Byron, who has five brothers and sisters

    Ⓑ   Mr. Barnes, who lives by himself

    Ⓒ   Connie, who works in a busy restaurant

    Ⓓ   Mrs. Diaz, who has a husband and three children

19. Which describes an <u>invasion</u>?

    Ⓐ   Calvin's sister calls him on the phone.

    Ⓑ   Calvin's sister reads his private diary.

    Ⓒ   Calvin invites his sister to lunch.

    Ⓓ   Calvin shares a room with his sister.

20. Which phrase describes an <u>impact</u>?

    Ⓐ   a book about meteors

    Ⓑ   a meteor in outer space

    Ⓒ   a meteor hitting the earth

    Ⓓ   a scientist who studies meteors

21. On whom can you <u>depend</u>?

    Ⓐ   Hattie, who is unreliable

    Ⓑ   Inara, who is reliable

    Ⓒ   Joe, who is lazy

    Ⓓ   Karen, who is never on time

22. Which of these might <u>appall</u> someone?

    Ⓐ   a cute kitten

    Ⓑ   new clothes

    Ⓒ   news of a car accident

    Ⓓ   an overdue library book

23. Our plans <u>depend</u> on the weather. What does this mean?

    Ⓐ   Our plans affect the weather.

    Ⓑ   Our plans cause changes in the weather.

    Ⓒ   Our plans are based on what the weather is.

    Ⓓ   Our plans will definitely be ruined by the weather.

24. I <u>suspect</u> that they have an excellent track team. What does <u>suspect</u> mean in this sentence?

    Ⓐ   I seriously doubt it.

    Ⓑ   I suppose it is true.

    Ⓒ   I am positive.

    Ⓓ   I do not believe it.

For items 25–30, find the word that means about the SAME as the underlined word. Then fill in the circle next to your answer.

25. <u>appalling</u>

    Ⓐ   exciting

    Ⓑ   fascinating

    Ⓒ   exhausting

    Ⓓ   shocking

26. <u>dejected</u>

    Ⓐ   sleepy

    Ⓑ   discouraged

    Ⓒ   envious

    Ⓓ   bored

27. <u>dependable</u>

    Ⓐ   reliable

    Ⓑ   intelligent

    Ⓒ   generous

    Ⓓ   kind

28. <u>invade</u>

    Ⓐ   injure

    Ⓑ   intrude

    Ⓒ   slay

    Ⓓ   steal

29. <u>occupation</u>

    Ⓐ   family

    Ⓑ   home

    Ⓒ   friends

    Ⓓ   job

30. <u>reveal</u>

    Ⓐ   glimpse

    Ⓑ   suspect

    Ⓒ   disclose

    Ⓓ   discover

For items 31–34, find the word that means the OPPOSITE of the underlined word. Then fill in the circle next to your answer.

31. <u>temporary</u>

    Ⓐ   short

    Ⓑ   helpful

    Ⓒ   annual

    Ⓓ   lasting

32. <u>dreary</u>

    Ⓐ   calm

    Ⓑ   cold

    Ⓒ   young

    Ⓓ   cheerful

33. <u>reveal</u>

    Ⓐ   agree

    Ⓑ   argue

    Ⓒ   hide

    Ⓓ   discover

34. <u>rout</u>

    Ⓐ   argument

    Ⓑ   disaster

    Ⓒ   war

    Ⓓ   victory

Book 4, Lesson 14 Test

Choose the BEST way to complete each sentence or answer each question. Then fill in the circle next to your answer.

1. A <u>chord</u> is

   Ⓐ   one musical note.

   Ⓑ   a musical instrument.

   Ⓒ   a musician in a large orchestra.

   Ⓓ   three or more musical notes played together.

2. A <u>humble</u> home is

   Ⓐ   large and beautiful.

   Ⓑ   plain and simple.

   Ⓒ   located outside of a city.

   Ⓓ   located in a city center.

3. To be <u>humbled</u> by an opponent is to

   Ⓐ   be brought to defeat.

   Ⓑ   play a game against him or her.

   Ⓒ   believe you are a better player than him or her.

   Ⓓ   be injured during a game.

4. The third time we asked if we could go to the party, Dad <u>relented</u>. Dad decided to

   Ⓐ   send us to our rooms.

   Ⓑ   go shopping.

   Ⓒ   make dinner.

   Ⓓ   let us go after all.

5. Mr. Powell cannot <u>afford</u> a new computer. He is not able to

   Ⓐ   pay for one.

   Ⓑ   find one that he likes.

   Ⓒ   understand how computers work.

   Ⓓ   connect to the Internet.

6. Stan can't <u>afford</u> to miss any more school days. This means that he

    Ⓐ   doesn't want to miss any more.

    Ⓑ   isn't able to miss any more.

    Ⓒ   has never been absent from school.

    Ⓓ   won't mind if he misses a few more days.

7. Reading <u>affords</u> me great pleasure. This means that reading

    Ⓐ   gives me great pleasure.

    Ⓑ   takes time away from other activities.

    Ⓒ   reminds me of happy times in the past.

    Ⓓ   used to be fun for me, but isn't anymore.

8. Our city <u>boasts</u> an excellent community center. This means that our city

    Ⓐ   plans to close the community center.

    Ⓑ   is proud of the community center that we have.

    Ⓒ   hopes to improve our community center.

    Ⓓ   plans to build another community center.

9. Amelia stood at the <u>fringe</u> of the group. Where did Amelia stand?

    Ⓐ   in the middle of the group.

    Ⓑ   across the room from the group.

    Ⓒ   at the edge of the group.

    Ⓓ   facing the group.

10. Albert <u>plunged</u> into the pool. He

    Ⓐ   threw himself into the pool.

    Ⓑ   ran toward the pool.

    Ⓒ   was afraid to go in the pool.

    Ⓓ   thought about jumping in the pool.

11. Carla <u>plunged</u> her hands into the bread dough. She

    Ⓐ   rolled a ball of dough in her hands.

    Ⓑ   patted the dough with her hands.

    Ⓒ   pushed her hands into the dough.

    Ⓓ   flattened the dough with her hands.

12. After the heat wave, the temperature <u>plunged</u>. What happened?

    Ⓐ   It got even hotter.

    Ⓑ   The temperature suddenly dropped.

    Ⓒ   The temperature gradually dropped.

    Ⓓ   The temperature gradually rose.

13. Salvador <u>submitted</u> a drawing to the judges of the art contest.

    Ⓐ   Salvador liked a drawing he saw in the contest.

    Ⓑ   Salvador was a judge in the art contest.

    Ⓒ   Salvador gave his drawing to the judges to look at.

    Ⓓ   Salvador told the judges not to choose his drawing.

14. June never <u>submits</u> to bullies. June

    Ⓐ   never talks to bullies.

    Ⓑ   never disagrees with bullies.

    Ⓒ   never eats lunch with bullies.

    Ⓓ   never gives in to bullies.

15. Which is most likely to <u>trudge</u> along?

    Ⓐ   a mouse escaping from a cat

    Ⓑ   a man walking through the snow in heavy boots

    Ⓒ   a dog running across a wood floor

    Ⓓ   a woman walking down a hallway in high-heeled shoes

16. If a judge asks, "How do you <u>plead</u>?" which answer makes sense?

    Ⓐ   "Not guilty, Your Honor."

    Ⓑ   "I'm fine, thank you."

    Ⓒ   "Please may I be excused?"

    Ⓓ   "My name is Kim Wynn."

17. Which is a <u>boast</u>?

    Ⓐ   "Are you on the track team?"

    Ⓑ   "We have a big meet tomorrow."

    Ⓒ   "I'm the best runner on the team!"

    Ⓓ   "I wish you wouldn't brag so much!"

18. Which is most likely to be decorated with <u>fringe</u>?

    Ⓐ   a chocolate cake

    Ⓑ   a leather jacket

    Ⓒ   a coffee mug

    Ⓓ   a new car

For items 19–23, find the word that means about the SAME as the underlined word. Then fill in the circle next to your answer.

19. <u>boast</u>

    Ⓐ   explain

    Ⓑ   bore

    Ⓒ   brag

    Ⓓ   teach

20. <u>meadow</u>

    Ⓐ   path

    Ⓑ   flowerbed

    Ⓒ   backyard

    Ⓓ   field

21. <u>obstinate</u>

    Ⓐ   lazy

    Ⓑ   stubborn

    Ⓒ   sneaky

    Ⓓ   impolite

22. <u>plead</u>

    Ⓐ   beg

    Ⓑ   command

    Ⓒ   request

    Ⓓ   instruct

23. <u>melancholy</u>

    Ⓐ   joy

    Ⓑ   fury

    Ⓒ   sorrow

    Ⓓ   boredom

For items 24–28, find the word that means the OPPOSITE of the underlined word. Then fill in the circle next to your answer.

24. <u>exceptional</u>

   Ⓐ smooth

   Ⓑ cool

   Ⓒ ordinary

   Ⓓ pale

25. <u>fortunate</u>

   Ⓐ melancholy

   Ⓑ obstinate

   Ⓒ intelligent

   Ⓓ unlucky

26. <u>humble</u>

   Ⓐ unfriendly

   Ⓑ proud

   Ⓒ envious

   Ⓓ crafty

27. <u>melancholy</u>

   Ⓐ joyful

   Ⓑ shiny

   Ⓒ silky

   Ⓓ sad

28. <u>plunge</u>

   Ⓐ expand

   Ⓑ lengthen

   Ⓒ widen

   Ⓓ rise

Name: _____ Date: _____

Book 4, Lesson 15 Test

Choose the BEST way to complete each sentence or answer each question. Then fill in the circle next to your answer.

1. A <u>ban</u> on smoking is

   Ⓐ   an illness that some smokers get.

   Ⓑ   a place where smoking is permitted.

   Ⓒ   a law or rule that forbids smoking.

   Ⓓ   a pack of cigarettes.

2. To <u>concentrate</u> on a math problem is to

   Ⓐ   solve it.

   Ⓑ   focus on it.

   Ⓒ   ask a question about it.

   Ⓓ   discuss it.

3. <u>Concentrated</u> apple juice

   Ⓐ   is stronger than regular apple juice.

   Ⓑ   has chunks of apple in it.

   Ⓒ   tastes better than regular apple juice.

   Ⓓ   has gone bad.

4. To <u>consider</u> a problem is to

   Ⓐ   solve it.

   Ⓑ   cause it.

   Ⓒ   think about it.

   Ⓓ   forget about it.

5. To <u>consider</u> yourself ready for middle school is to

   Ⓐ   believe you are ready.

   Ⓑ   worry that you are not ready.

   Ⓒ   hope you will be ready.

   Ⓓ   get yourself ready.

6. To <u>contrast</u> two movies is to

    Ⓐ   show how they are different.

    Ⓑ   show how they are similar.

    Ⓒ   try to choose which one to see.

    Ⓓ   have difficulty choosing one or the other.

7. The kitten <u>pounced</u> on a ball of yarn. The kitten

    Ⓐ   glimpsed the ball of yarn.

    Ⓑ   jumped on and seized the ball of yarn.

    Ⓒ   unraveled the ball of yarn.

    Ⓓ   got tangled in the ball of yarn.

8. Aliyah's e-mail message <u>prompted</u> me to call her. What did the e-mail message do?

    Ⓐ   It caused me to call.

    Ⓑ   It worried me.

    Ⓒ   It puzzled me.

    Ⓓ   It came right after I called Aliyah.

9. Lack of sleep is the <u>apparent</u> reason for Steve's irritability. Lack of sleep

    Ⓐ   is one of the reasons.

    Ⓑ   is not the reason.

    Ⓒ   is probably not the reason.

    Ⓓ   appears to be the reason.

10. Ants have <u>concentrated</u> around your spilled ice cream. They have

    Ⓐ   come together around the ice cream.

    Ⓑ   spread out all over.

    Ⓒ   wandered away from the ice cream.

    Ⓓ   eaten all the ice cream.

11. If your friend says "You broke my <u>concentration</u>!" what does he mean?

    Ⓐ   You wasted your time.

    Ⓑ   You kept him from paying attention.

    Ⓒ   You helped him with a chore.

    Ⓓ   You injured him.

12. There is an article <u>concerning</u> Rosa Parks in the school newspaper. The article

    Ⓐ   is written by Rosa Parks.

    Ⓑ   is about Rosa Parks.

    Ⓒ   tells about Rosa Parks' worries.

    Ⓓ   tells about Rosa Parks' family.

13. Ms. Butterfield owns a frozen foods <u>concern</u>. This means that she

    Ⓐ   cooks with frozen foods.

    Ⓑ   has a frozen foods company.

    Ⓒ   bought some frozen foods.

    Ⓓ   wrote a frozen foods cookbook.

14. Education is an important <u>concern</u>. In this sentence, <u>concern</u> means

    Ⓐ   a goal.

    Ⓑ   a problem.

    Ⓒ   an issue that involves many people.

    Ⓓ   an issue that people often ignore.

15. If your father says, "Please <u>consider</u> your little brother's feelings," what does he mean?

    Ⓐ   Take account of your brother's feelings.

    Ⓑ   Tell someone about your brother's feelings.

    Ⓒ   Don't worry about your brother's feelings.

    Ⓓ   Talk with your brother about his feelings.

16. Yusef's plans for the weekend <u>contrast</u> with Margot's plans. What does this tell you about their plans?

    Ⓐ   They are different.

    Ⓑ   They are the same.

    Ⓒ   They are almost the same.

    Ⓓ   They are exciting.

17. My new school is a <u>contrast</u> to my old one. This means that my new school is

    Ⓐ   better than my old one.

    Ⓑ   worse than my old one.

    Ⓒ   different from my old one.

    Ⓓ   far away from my old one.

18. A <u>widespread</u> problem is one that

    Ⓐ   two people share.

    Ⓑ   no one can solve.

    Ⓒ   has been solved.

    Ⓓ   many people share.

19. Which is most likely to <u>menace</u> a driver?

    Ⓐ   a traffic signal

    Ⓑ   a stop sign

    Ⓒ   an icy road

    Ⓓ   a speed limit

20. Grandpa welcomed Shelby with <u>widespread</u> arms. How was Grandpa holding his arms?

    Ⓐ   stretched wide open

    Ⓑ   above his head

    Ⓒ   folded across his chest

    Ⓓ   against his sides

21. Which has <u>talons</u>?

    Ⓐ   a cow

    Ⓑ   a horse

    Ⓒ   an eagle

    Ⓓ   an elephant

22. Which is an addition <u>symbol</u>?

    Ⓐ   adding

    Ⓑ   +

    Ⓒ   subtraction

    Ⓓ   Two plus three equals five.

23. Which of the following is most <u>recent</u>?

    Ⓐ   yesterday

    Ⓑ   last week

    Ⓒ   last month

    Ⓓ   last year

For items 24–27, find the word that means about the SAME as the underlined word. Then fill in the circle next to your answer.

24. <u>apparent</u>

    Ⓐ   clear

    Ⓑ   fascinating

    Ⓒ   boring

    Ⓓ   complicated

25. <u>concerned</u>

    Ⓐ   angry

    Ⓑ   content

    Ⓒ   confused

    Ⓓ   worried

26. <u>trophy</u>

    Ⓐ   contest

    Ⓑ   prize

    Ⓒ   winner

    Ⓓ   loser

27. <u>menace</u>

    Ⓐ   safety

    Ⓑ   danger

    Ⓒ   volunteer

    Ⓓ   neighbor

For items 28–30, find the word that means the OPPOSITE of the underlined word. Then fill in the circle next to your answer.

28. <u>ban</u>

    Ⓐ   allow

    Ⓑ   teach

    Ⓒ   nourish

    Ⓓ   shelter

29. <u>fragile</u>

    Ⓐ warm

    Ⓑ smooth

    Ⓒ strong

    Ⓓ cozy

30. <u>prompt</u>

    Ⓐ mischievous

    Ⓑ lazy

    Ⓒ stubborn

    Ⓓ late

Book 4, Lesson 16 Test

Choose the BEST way to complete each sentence or answer each question. Then fill in the circle next to your answer.

1. When a tree <u>blossoms</u>, it

   Ⓐ   dies.

   Ⓑ   forms buds.

   Ⓒ   loses its leaves.

   Ⓓ   blooms.

2. I'm <u>apt</u> to forget people's names. What does <u>apt</u> mean in this sentence?

   Ⓐ   likely

   Ⓑ   not likely

   Ⓒ   embarrassed

   Ⓓ   skilled

3. How would you probably feel about a <u>detestable</u> idea?

   Ⓐ   You would not care about it.

   Ⓑ   You would be surprised by it.

   Ⓒ   You would strongly dislike it.

   Ⓓ   You would love it.

4. Which of the following grows in an <u>orchard</u>?

   Ⓐ   corn

   Ⓑ   rice

   Ⓒ   fruit trees

   Ⓓ   horses

5. I'm <u>familiar</u> with this joke. This means that I

   Ⓐ   am excited about hearing it.

   Ⓑ   already know it.

   Ⓒ   plan to tell it soon.

   Ⓓ   do not think it's funny.

6. To <u>practice</u> good eating habits is to

- (A) perform good eating habits.
- (B) perform bad eating habits.
- (C) eat too much.
- (D) eat too little.

7. To <u>practice</u> medicine is to

- (A) work in the medical field.
- (B) take medicine for an illness.
- (C) learn about medicine in school.
- (D) buy medicine in a drugstore.

8. To <u>prune</u> a tree is to

- (A) water it.
- (B) plant it.
- (C) cut it down for firewood.
- (D) cut off some of its branches.

9. What is a <u>prune</u>?

- (A) a raisin
- (B) a fig
- (C) a dried plum
- (D) a dried apple

10. It is my uncle's <u>practice</u> to bike to work every day. In this sentence, <u>practice</u> means

- (A) chore.
- (B) usual way of doing something.
- (C) harsh punishment.
- (D) profession.

11. The <u>practice</u> of law is harder than it seems on television. What does <u>practice</u> mean in this sentence?

- (A) profession
- (B) crime
- (C) rules
- (D) actors

12. Petra's mind began to <u>wander</u> from her math problems. What happened?

- Ⓐ Petra walked out of her math class.
- Ⓑ Petra began to concentrate on math.
- Ⓒ Petra was not concentrating on math anymore.
- Ⓓ Petra thought about traveling.

13. Rodney <u>blossomed</u> into a world-class chef. This means that he

- Ⓐ bumped into a world-class chef.
- Ⓑ knew a world-class chef.
- Ⓒ developed into a world-class chef.
- Ⓓ wasn't quite old enough to be a world-class chef.

14. Which of these is the OPPOSITE of <u>wandering</u>?

- Ⓐ practicing every day
- Ⓑ settling down in one place
- Ⓒ behaving well
- Ⓓ receiving a high score

15. Jeremy has to be home by <u>dusk</u>. At what time should he go home?

- Ⓐ 9 a.m.
- Ⓑ 12 p.m.
- Ⓒ 5 p.m.
- Ⓓ 11 p.m.

16. What does "<u>practice</u> makes perfect" mean?

- Ⓐ If you do something over and over, you will become good at it.
- Ⓑ If you like doing something, you will want to practice.
- Ⓒ If you cannot do something perfectly, you should not do it at all.
- Ⓓ Nobody is perfect.

For items 17–22, find the word that means about the SAME as the underlined word. Then fill in the circle next to your answer.

17. <u>blossom</u>

- Ⓐ grass
- Ⓑ tree
- Ⓒ flower
- Ⓓ honeybee

18. <u>bough</u>

    Ⓐ leaf

    Ⓑ twig

    Ⓒ trunk

    Ⓓ branch

19. <u>contentment</u>

    Ⓐ satisfaction

    Ⓑ laziness

    Ⓒ boredom

    Ⓓ curiosity

20. <u>threadbare</u>

    Ⓐ smooth

    Ⓑ shabby

    Ⓒ colorful

    Ⓓ filthy

21. <u>detest</u>

    Ⓐ hate

    Ⓑ destroy

    Ⓒ fear

    Ⓓ flee

22. <u>stout</u>

    Ⓐ wooden

    Ⓑ strong

    Ⓒ stone

    Ⓓ short

For items 23–28, find the word that means the OPPOSITE of the underlined word. Then fill in the circle next to your answer.

23. <u>content</u>

    Ⓐ crafty

    Ⓑ warlike

    Ⓒ curious

    Ⓓ dissatisfied

24. <u>obtain</u>

    Ⓐ   begin

    Ⓑ   lose

    Ⓒ   receive

    Ⓓ   help

25. <u>extinguish</u>

    Ⓐ   freeze

    Ⓑ   finish

    Ⓒ   cook

    Ⓓ   light

26. <u>stout</u>

    Ⓐ   pretty

    Ⓑ   lively

    Ⓒ   skinny

    Ⓓ   smooth

27. <u>apt</u>

    Ⓐ   unusual

    Ⓑ   unsuitable

    Ⓒ   exact

    Ⓓ   boring

28. <u>familiar</u>

    Ⓐ   strange

    Ⓑ   rough

    Ⓒ   icy

    Ⓓ   comfortable

Copyright protected by Educators Publishing Service. Permission is granted to reproduce this page

Book 4, Lesson 17 Test

Choose the BEST way to complete each sentence or answer each question. Then fill in the circle next to your answer.

1. To <u>address</u> a group of people is to

   Ⓐ speak to them.

   Ⓑ listen to them.

   Ⓒ lead them.

   Ⓓ send them a letter.

2. The student council president says that she will <u>address</u> all of our concerns. What does she mean?

   Ⓐ She will agree with our concerns.

   Ⓑ She will apply herself to our concerns.

   Ⓒ She will not worry about our concerns.

   Ⓓ She will ignore our concerns.

3. There was excellent French and Italian <u>fare</u> at the international club's party. What does <u>fare</u> mean in this sentence?

   Ⓐ music

   Ⓑ decorations

   Ⓒ dancing

   Ⓓ food

4. A <u>hearty</u> meal is

   Ⓐ small but delicious.

   Ⓑ unhealthy.

   Ⓒ expensive.

   Ⓓ large and satisfying.

5. Which of the following could be the train <u>fare</u> from New York to Washington, D.C.?

   Ⓐ 250 miles

   Ⓑ 5 hours

   Ⓒ 50 dollars

   Ⓓ 7 cars

6. Our science teacher <u>escorted</u> us through the museum. What does <u>escorted</u> mean in this sentence?

    Ⓐ   left us alone

    Ⓑ   organized

    Ⓒ   guided

    Ⓓ   reminded us to be quiet

7. Mr. Abrams <u>concluded</u> that this movie is not worth seeing. In this sentence, <u>concluded</u> means

    Ⓐ   told people.

    Ⓑ   felt sorry.

    Ⓒ   formed an opinion.

    Ⓓ   disagreed.

8. Sarah's parents <u>approve</u> of her friends. Sarah's parents

    Ⓐ   dislike her friends.

    Ⓑ   like her friends.

    Ⓒ   think her friends are impolite.

    Ⓓ   think her friends are noisy.

9. Derek values his grandmother's <u>approval</u>. He wants his grandmother to

    Ⓐ   think well of him.

    Ⓑ   invite him over for dinner.

    Ⓒ   stop working so hard.

    Ⓓ   exercise and eat healthy foods.

10. Alexa came to the <u>conclusion</u> that peanut butter and ketchup do not go well together. In this sentence, <u>conclusion</u> means

    Ⓐ   ending.

    Ⓑ   judgment.

    Ⓒ   complaint.

    Ⓓ   information.

11. I think your plan has <u>merit</u>. In this sentence, <u>merit</u> means

    Ⓐ   supporters.

    Ⓑ   complications.

    Ⓒ   worth.

    Ⓓ   problems.

12. A jury should decide a court case based upon its <u>merits</u>. In this sentence, <u>merits</u> means

- Ⓐ facts.
- Ⓑ judgments.
- Ⓒ victims.
- Ⓓ opinions.

13. Emma <u>summoned</u> all her strength to finish the race. In this sentence, <u>summoned</u> means

- Ⓐ gathered together.
- Ⓑ worried about.
- Ⓒ did not need.
- Ⓓ saved.

14. A village council of <u>elders</u> is a group of

- Ⓐ children who receive care and education from their neighbors.
- Ⓑ people whom others respect for their age and experience.
- Ⓒ young people who help their neighbors with chores.
- Ⓓ adults who meet to play sports and games.

15. Which is an <u>address</u>?

- Ⓐ (415) 555-1212
- Ⓑ 1000 San Pablo Avenue
- Ⓒ 10 years old
- Ⓓ Warner Elementary School

16. The teacher asked, "How did you <u>fare</u> on the test?" What did she mean?

- Ⓐ How did you do on the test?
- Ⓑ Did you study for the test?
- Ⓒ Are you finished with your test?
- Ⓓ Did you write your name on your test?

For items 17–24, find the word that means about the SAME as the underlined word. Then fill in the circle next to your answer.

17. <u>address</u>

- Ⓐ request
- Ⓑ word
- Ⓒ speech
- Ⓓ warning

18. <u>elder</u>

    Ⓐ younger

    Ⓑ richer

    Ⓒ older

    Ⓓ poorer

19. <u>escort</u>

    Ⓐ servant

    Ⓑ guide

    Ⓒ relative

    Ⓓ teammate

20. <u>hearty</u>

    Ⓐ friendly

    Ⓑ boring

    Ⓒ fascinating

    Ⓓ sorrowful

21. <u>merited</u>

    Ⓐ obtained

    Ⓑ deserved

    Ⓒ used

    Ⓓ provided

22. <u>concluded</u>

    Ⓐ led

    Ⓑ continued

    Ⓒ ended

    Ⓓ organized

23. <u>waft</u>

    Ⓐ drift

    Ⓑ paddle

    Ⓒ race

    Ⓓ scurry

24. <u>forlorn</u>

    Ⓐ furious

    Ⓑ lonely

    Ⓒ joyful

    Ⓓ irritable

For items 25–32, find the word that means the OPPOSITE of the underlined word. Then fill in the circle next to your answer.

25. <u>conclusion</u>

    Ⓐ beginning

    Ⓑ dusk

    Ⓒ midpoint

    Ⓓ ending

26. <u>elder</u>

    Ⓐ youngster

    Ⓑ grandparent

    Ⓒ brother

    Ⓓ sister

27. <u>inhaling</u>

    Ⓐ gasping

    Ⓑ raining

    Ⓒ blowing

    Ⓓ crying

28. <u>stingy</u>

    Ⓐ comfortable

    Ⓑ generous

    Ⓒ greedy

    Ⓓ contented

29. <u>summon</u>

    Ⓐ request

    Ⓑ command

    Ⓒ assign

    Ⓓ dismiss

30. <u>hearty</u>

    Ⓐ smooth

    Ⓑ weak

    Ⓒ short

    Ⓓ young

31. <u>valiant</u>

    Ⓐ grouchy

    Ⓑ forlorn

    Ⓒ mournful

    Ⓓ cowardly

32. <u>deprive</u>

    Ⓐ wander

    Ⓑ greet

    Ⓒ give

    Ⓓ excuse

Book 4, Lesson 18 Test

Choose the BEST way to complete each sentence or answer each question. Then fill in the circle next to your answer.

1. The director instructed us to stand five <u>abreast</u> on stage. She instructed us to stand

   Ⓐ   in height order.

   Ⓑ   side-by-side.

   Ⓒ   in a circle.

   Ⓓ   clustered together.

2. To stay <u>abreast</u> of current events means to

   Ⓐ   avoid watching the news.

   Ⓑ   comment on current events.

   Ⓒ   keep up-to-date on current events.

   Ⓓ   be featured in the news.

3. A <u>capital</u> crime is

   Ⓐ   punishable by death.

   Ⓑ   one with no victims.

   Ⓒ   done by accident.

   Ⓓ   punishable by community service.

4. To <u>ensure</u> someone's safety is to

   Ⓐ   be certain that person is safe.

   Ⓑ   discuss that person's safety.

   Ⓒ   worry about that person's safety.

   Ⓓ   warn that person about danger.

5. A <u>feud</u> is a

   Ⓐ   long journey.

   Ⓑ   long period of bad weather.

   Ⓒ   long, close friendship.

   Ⓓ   long, bitter quarrel.

6. To <u>frequent</u> the mall is to

  Ⓐ go there again and again.

  Ⓑ drive there.

  Ⓒ work there.

  Ⓓ go there occasionally.

7. A <u>frontier</u> is the line between

  Ⓐ two halves of a circle.

  Ⓑ two countries.

  Ⓒ neighbors' homes.

  Ⓓ two halves of a football field.

8. Ms. Patel was very impressed with Simon's <u>breadth</u> of knowledge. What does <u>breadth</u> mean in this sentence?

  Ⓐ magazine articles

  Ⓑ attitude toward

  Ⓒ wide range

  Ⓓ love

9. Tamara <u>threatened</u> that she would take away her sister's radio if she did not turn it down. In this sentence, what does <u>threatened</u> mean?

  Ⓐ screamed

  Ⓑ warned

  Ⓒ told her parents

  Ⓓ lied

10. A <u>peasant</u>

  Ⓐ is a king or queen.

  Ⓑ is a prince or princess.

  Ⓒ makes a living from working the soil.

  Ⓓ makes a living from raising cattle.

11. Which of the following is a <u>frontier</u>?

  Ⓐ the southern part of a country

  Ⓑ the capital city of a country

  Ⓒ the population of a large country

  Ⓓ the outer limits of a settled country

12. Which describes the <u>frontiers</u> of science?

    Ⓐ   the outer limits of scientific knowledge

    Ⓑ   brilliant scientists

    Ⓒ   chemistry, biology, and physics

    Ⓓ   scientific formulas

13. Which describes <u>threatening</u> weather?

    Ⓐ   cool and clear

    Ⓑ   sunny and warm

    Ⓒ   dark and cloudy

    Ⓓ   gently drizzling

14. Which is a <u>threat</u>?

    Ⓐ   "Please don't walk across my lawn."

    Ⓑ   "If you walk across my lawn, I will tell your mom."

    Ⓒ   "Please be careful as you walk across the street."

    Ⓓ   "You must follow all safety rules."

15. Which of the following is a <u>frequency</u>?

    Ⓐ   two years until middle school

    Ⓑ   eleven years old

    Ⓒ   three times per week

    Ⓓ   eighty pounds

16. Which is a <u>capital</u>?

    Ⓐ   Mt. Everest

    Ⓑ   Asia

    Ⓒ   Paris, France

    Ⓓ   the Pacific Ocean

17. Who is most likely to need <u>capital</u>?

    Ⓐ   a child in preschool

    Ⓑ   a student who is graduating from elementary school

    Ⓒ   a family pet

    Ⓓ   a businessperson who is opening a new store

18. Which is most likely to be a <u>barrier</u> to a friendship?

    Ⓐ   having an argument

    Ⓑ   having the same hobbies

    Ⓒ   being neighbors

    Ⓓ   being in the same class

For items 19–23, find the word that means about the SAME as the underlined word. Then fill in the circle next to your answer.

19. <u>breadth</u>

    Ⓐ   length

    Ⓑ   width

    Ⓒ   height

    Ⓓ   depth

20. <u>external</u>

    Ⓐ   attractive

    Ⓑ   strong

    Ⓒ   protective

    Ⓓ   outside

21. <u>feuding</u>

    Ⓐ   discussing

    Ⓑ   organizing

    Ⓒ   quarreling

    Ⓓ   mentioning

22. <u>fortress</u>

    Ⓐ   mansion

    Ⓑ   fort

    Ⓒ   skyscraper

    Ⓓ   mountain

23. <u>utilized</u>

    Ⓐ   wasted

    Ⓑ   requested

    Ⓒ   used

    Ⓓ   inquired

For items 24–26, find the word that means the OPPOSITE of the underlined word. Then fill in the circle next to your answer.

24. <u>frequent</u>

    Ⓐ   rare

    Ⓑ   fragrant

    Ⓒ   exquisite

    Ⓓ   strange

25. <u>petty</u>

    Ⓐ   complicated

    Ⓑ   important

    Ⓒ   irritating

    Ⓓ   finicky

26. <u>vast</u>

    Ⓐ   cute

    Ⓑ   friendly

    Ⓒ   silky

    Ⓓ   small

Name: _____   Date: _____

Book 4, Lesson 19 Test

Choose the BEST way to complete each sentence or answer each question. Then fill in the circle next to your answer.

1. To <u>create</u> a computer program is to

   Ⓐ play one.

   Ⓑ buy one.

   Ⓒ understand one.

   Ⓓ make one.

2. Which of the following is a <u>trio</u>?

   Ⓐ a group of two people

   Ⓑ a group of three people

   Ⓒ a group of four people

   Ⓓ a group of five people

3. When a couple becomes <u>engaged</u>, the two people agree to

   Ⓐ buy a house.

   Ⓑ get married.

   Ⓒ act in a play.

   Ⓓ take a vacation.

4. To <u>forsake</u> a friend is to

   Ⓐ make a new friend.

   Ⓑ give your friend a birthday gift.

   Ⓒ turn your back on your friend.

   Ⓓ send your friend a letter.

5. <u>Essentials</u> are items that someone

   Ⓐ has lost.

   Ⓑ cannot do without.

   Ⓒ can give as gifts.

   Ⓓ has discovered for the first time.

Wordly Wise 3000 Book

6. A river's <u>source</u> is

   Ⓐ   the place where it starts.

   Ⓑ   the place where it joins another river.

   Ⓒ   its width.

   Ⓓ   its length.

7. The kaleidoscope <u>engaged</u> the baby for an entire hour. Which of the following is probably true?

   Ⓐ   The kaleidoscope bored the baby.

   Ⓑ   The kaleidoscope kept the baby busy.

   Ⓒ   The kaleidoscope frightened the baby.

   Ⓓ   The kaleidoscope surprised the baby.

8. The new puppy <u>entranced</u> Tomás. The puppy made Tomás feel

   Ⓐ   jealous.

   Ⓑ   irritated.

   Ⓒ   nervous.

   Ⓓ   delighted.

9. <u>Elimination</u> is the process of

   Ⓐ   getting started.

   Ⓑ   getting ready.

   Ⓒ   getting rid of something.

   Ⓓ   getting organized.

10. To <u>recognize</u> someone's good work is to

   Ⓐ   take credit for that person's work.

   Ⓑ   accept and approve of that person's work.

   Ⓒ   help that person with their work.

   Ⓓ   tell that person to work harder.

11. To <u>tour</u> Nepal is to

   Ⓐ   read about Nepal.

   Ⓑ   travel to the different places in Nepal.

   Ⓒ   write to someone who lives in Nepal.

   Ⓓ   study the culture of Nepal.

12. A <u>sentimental</u> movie is most likely to be

 Ⓐ a horror movie

 Ⓑ an action movie

 Ⓒ a true story

 Ⓓ a love story

13. A <u>creative</u> person is someone with

 Ⓐ strong muscles.

 Ⓑ wealth and power.

 Ⓒ new and original ideas.

 Ⓓ many friends and family members.

14. People hold <u>auditions</u> to choose

 Ⓐ actors for new plays.

 Ⓑ new homes.

 Ⓒ new pets.

 Ⓓ lawyers for court cases.

15. I <u>recognized</u> Aimee right away. I

 Ⓐ called Aimee immediately.

 Ⓑ remembered Aimee as soon as I saw her.

 Ⓒ made friends with Aimee very quickly.

 Ⓓ paid Aimee the money I owed her.

16. Mr. Cohen <u>recognized</u> that he was defeated and gracefully stepped out of the race. What does <u>recognized</u> mean in this sentence?

 Ⓐ accepted

 Ⓑ denied

 Ⓒ was angry

 Ⓓ was relieved

17. Some say that J. K. Rowling is the world's <u>foremost</u> children's author. In this sentence, <u>foremost</u> means

 Ⓐ oldest.

 Ⓑ most important.

 Ⓒ youngest.

 Ⓓ funniest.

18. This product contains eight <u>essential</u> vitamins and minerals. In this sentence, <u>essential</u> means

    Ⓐ   common.

    Ⓑ   unusual.

    Ⓒ   necessary.

    Ⓓ   delicious.

19. What is a <u>traditional</u> story?

    Ⓐ   a story in a magazine

    Ⓑ   a story that is handed down from age to age

    Ⓒ   a story that has a happy ending

    Ⓓ   a story that expresses feelings of love or pity

20. The <u>creation</u> of a comic strip is

    Ⓐ   the author of the comic strip.

    Ⓑ   the newspaper that prints the comic strip.

    Ⓒ   when the comic strip came into being.

    Ⓓ   when the comic strip stopped being printed.

21. Which is an <u>elevation</u>?

    Ⓐ   5,000 feet above sea level

    Ⓑ   5,000 pounds

    Ⓒ   5,000 years

    Ⓓ   5,000 dollars

22. Who or what <u>auditions</u> for an orchestra?

    Ⓐ   a musical instrument

    Ⓑ   a musician

    Ⓒ   an audience

    Ⓓ   a concert

For items 23–28, find the word that means about the SAME as the underlined word. Then fill in the circle next to your answer.

23. <u>tour</u>

    Ⓐ   errand

    Ⓑ   journey

    Ⓒ   accident

    Ⓓ   tower

24. <u>tradition</u>

    Ⓐ   suggestion

    Ⓑ   command

    Ⓒ   request

    Ⓓ   custom

25. <u>elevated</u>

    Ⓐ   widened

    Ⓑ   raised

    Ⓒ   rotated

    Ⓓ   square

26. <u>eliminated</u>

    Ⓐ   polished

    Ⓑ   transformed

    Ⓒ   improved

    Ⓓ   removed

27. <u>engage</u>

    Ⓐ   meet

    Ⓑ   organize

    Ⓒ   hire

    Ⓓ   request

28. <u>entrancing</u>

    Ⓐ   confusing

    Ⓑ   delightful

    Ⓒ   surprising

    Ⓓ   calming

Book 4, Lesson 20 Test

Choose the BEST way to complete each sentence or answer each question. Then fill in the circle next to your answer.

1. When a police officer makes an <u>arrest</u>, she

    Ⓐ   learns how to drive a patrol car.

    Ⓑ   seizes someone who has broken a law.

    Ⓒ   helps a driver who has had an accident.

    Ⓓ   directs traffic.

2. Someone who is <u>capable of</u> becoming an artist

    Ⓐ   is too lazy to become an artist.

    Ⓑ   is ready and able to become an artist.

    Ⓒ   does not want to become an artist.

    Ⓓ   is already an artist.

3. "<u>Congratulations</u>!" means

    Ⓐ   "Hello!"

    Ⓑ   "Sweet dreams!"

    Ⓒ   "Please stop!"

    Ⓓ   "I'm happy for you!"

4. To <u>dispute</u> a fact is to

    Ⓐ   believe it is true.

    Ⓑ   find it on the Internet.

    Ⓒ   question it.

    Ⓓ   find it fascinating.

5. A <u>helm</u> is a wheel that steers

    Ⓐ   a boat.

    Ⓑ   a car.

    Ⓒ   a bicycle.

    Ⓓ   a train.

6. Someone who suffers <u>humiliation</u> feels

    Ⓐ   contented.

    Ⓑ   bored and gloomy.

    Ⓒ   very embarrassed.

    Ⓓ   exhausted.

7. A newspaper <u>insert</u> is

    Ⓐ   a regular article.

    Ⓑ   a newspaper delivery person.

    Ⓒ   an extra piece placed inside a newspaper.

    Ⓓ   a building where a newspaper has its headquarters.

8. An <u>outrage</u> is anything that causes

    Ⓐ   curiosity.

    Ⓑ   resentment.

    Ⓒ   confusion.

    Ⓓ   contentment.

9. A flashlight beam <u>pierced</u> the darkness. It

    Ⓐ   broke through the darkness.

    Ⓑ   was not visible.

    Ⓒ   pointed toward the ceiling.

    Ⓓ   moved in a big circle.

10. Someone with a <u>quiver</u> in his voice probably feels

    Ⓐ   self-confident.

    Ⓑ   peaceful and calm.

    Ⓒ   nervous or fearful.

    Ⓓ   quiet and contented.

11. What does a <u>quiver</u> hold?

    Ⓐ   money.

    Ⓑ   letters.

    Ⓒ   arrows.

    Ⓓ   eating utensils.

12. To <u>release</u> information is to

     Ⓐ   read about it.

     Ⓑ   write about it.

     Ⓒ   learn about it.

     Ⓓ   disclose it.

13. The innocent woman received a <u>release</u> from prison. A <u>release</u> is

     Ⓐ   a letter.

     Ⓑ   a visitor.

     Ⓒ   an arrest.

     Ⓓ   a setting free.

14. The principal <u>released</u> information about the new cafeteria menu. The principal

     Ⓐ   kept the information a secret.

     Ⓑ   made the information known.

     Ⓒ   did not have any information.

     Ⓓ   discovered new information.

15. To act <u>sullen</u> is to

     Ⓐ   be silent because you are angry.

     Ⓑ   be silent because you are shocked.

     Ⓒ   be silent because you have lost your voice.

     Ⓓ   be silent because you are tired.

16. How would you <u>pierce</u> a marshmallow?

     Ⓐ   roast it over a fire

     Ⓑ   put a stick through it

     Ⓒ   put it on a graham cracker

     Ⓓ   eat it

17. Which is most likely to cause <u>outrage</u>?

     Ⓐ   a bus ride

     Ⓑ   a delicious lunch

     Ⓒ   a crime

     Ⓓ   a school fair

18. The voice on the telephone says, "Please <u>insert</u> fifty cents." What should you do?

Ⓐ   make a call that costs fifty cents

Ⓑ   put fifty cents into the phone

Ⓒ   borrow fifty cents from someone

Ⓓ   send fifty cents to the phone company

19. Which is most likely to <u>humiliate</u> someone?

Ⓐ   greeting that person

Ⓑ   mocking that person

Ⓒ   helping that person with his or her homework

Ⓓ   waving goodbye to that person

20. Who is most likely to be at the <u>helm</u> of your school play?

Ⓐ   an actor

Ⓑ   a band member

Ⓒ   a set painter

Ⓓ   the director

21. When might you <u>congratulate</u> someone?

Ⓐ   when that person eats a sandwich for lunch

Ⓑ   when that person graduates

Ⓒ   when that person is late for school

Ⓓ   when that person goes to bed

22. Which is <u>capable</u> of traveling at eighty miles per hour?

Ⓐ   a tricycle

Ⓑ   a honeybee

Ⓒ   a car

Ⓓ   a mouse

23. Who is most likely to be <u>arrested</u>?

Ⓐ   a man walking his dog

Ⓑ   a suspected thief

Ⓒ   a grocery store shopper

Ⓓ   a woman making a phone call

For items 24–30, find the word that means about the SAME as the underlined word. Then fill in the circle next to your answer.

24. <u>arrested</u>

     Ⓐ explored

     Ⓑ improved

     Ⓒ stopped

     Ⓓ organized

25. <u>capable</u>

     Ⓐ skilled

     Ⓑ generous

     Ⓒ obedient

     Ⓓ loving

26. <u>dispute</u>

     Ⓐ discussion

     Ⓑ argument

     Ⓒ message

     Ⓓ conversation

27. <u>implored</u>

     Ⓐ begged

     Ⓑ commanded

     Ⓒ requested

     Ⓓ invited

28. <u>piercing</u>

     Ⓐ rhythmic

     Ⓑ deep

     Ⓒ shrill

     Ⓓ musical

29. <u>quivering</u>

     Ⓐ scratching

     Ⓑ trembling

     Ⓒ scurrying

     Ⓓ hopping

30. <u>outraged</u>

    Ⓐ   encouraged

    Ⓑ   irritated

    Ⓒ   bored

    Ⓓ   angered

For items 31–33, find the word that means the OPPOSITE of the underlined word. Then fill in the circle next to your answer.

31. <u>despise</u>

    Ⓐ   group

    Ⓑ   introduce

    Ⓒ   examine

    Ⓓ   respect

32. <u>eventual</u>

    Ⓐ   convenient

    Ⓑ   delicious

    Ⓒ   instant

    Ⓓ   attractive

33. <u>released</u>

    Ⓐ   captured

    Ⓑ   harmed

    Ⓒ   accused

    Ⓓ   despised

Name: _____   Date: _____

Book 4, Final Test 1 (Lessons 1–20)

Read the passage. Choose the BEST answer for each sentence or question about an underlined word. Then fill in the circle next to your answer.

OLD SAYINGS AND EXPRESSIONS, PART 1

English and other languages are filled with old sayings, expressions, and odd ways of putting words together. The meanings of some sayings are easy to figure out. For example: *It is better to be safe than sorry.* This means that people should be cautious. If they don't do their best to <u>ensure</u> their own and others' safety, they may be sorry later.

The meanings of other sayings are less <u>apparent</u>. For example: *It's a small world.* We all know that the world is a <u>vast</u> place. Why call it small? People use this saying to <u>remark</u> on amazing coincidences. For instance, let's say that your cousin Monique gets <u>engaged</u> to be married. Then you discover that Monique's husband-to-be is your best friend's Uncle Bill! You say, "Wow, it's a small world!" In other words—it turns out that we are more closely connected than we thought we were.

Many old sayings and expressions have to do with food. *Don't bite off more than you can chew*, for example. This means that if you are not <u>capable of</u> doing something, you shouldn't promise that you will. Then there's *Don't cry over spilled milk.* This means that you can't <u>alter</u> an event after it has already happened. It is no use <u>grieving</u> over something that you cannot change.

For some reason, eggs are a popular topic in old sayings and expressions. *He's a good egg means* "He's a good, reliable person." *Don't put all of your eggs in one basket means*, "Don't <u>depend</u> on just one person or just one solution to all of your problems." Have you ever heard someone say, "*There I sat with egg on my face*?" In other words, they felt <u>humiliated</u>.

Imagine trying to tread on eggs without breaking their <u>fragile</u> shells. This will help you to understand another egg-related expression. Someone might say, "Around Aunt Roberta, I'm always *walking on eggshells*." In other words, "I have to watch everything I say and do around Aunt Roberta! The slightest little thing could make her <u>furious</u>!"

1. Read this sentence from the passage.

   If they don't do their best to <u>ensure</u> their own and others' safety, they may be sorry later.

   To <u>ensure</u> someone's safety means to

   Ⓐ hope that person will be safe.

   Ⓑ worry about that person's careless behavior.

   Ⓒ make sure that person is safe.

   Ⓓ apologize to that person for careless behavior.

2. Read this sentence from the passage.

   The meanings of other sayings are less <u>apparent</u>.

   In this sentence, <u>apparent</u> means

   Ⓐ interesting.

   Ⓑ amusing.

   Ⓒ clear.

   Ⓓ complicated.

3. Read this sentence from the passage.

   The world is a <u>vast</u> place.

   This sentence means that the world is very

   Ⓐ large.

   Ⓑ beautiful.

   Ⓒ unpredictable.

   Ⓓ fascinating.

4. Read this sentence from the passage.

   People use this saying to <u>remark</u> on amazing coincidences.

   In this sentence, "<u>remark</u> on" means

   Ⓐ comment on.

   Ⓑ brag about.

   Ⓒ complain about.

   Ⓓ ask about.

5. Read this sentence from the passage.

Your cousin Monique gets <u>engaged</u> to be married.

Someone who is <u>engaged</u> to be married

- Ⓐ is newly married.
- Ⓑ is looking for someone to marry.
- Ⓒ has promised to marry someone.
- Ⓓ has relatives who are married.

6. Read this sentence from the passage.

If you are not <u>capable of</u> doing something, you shouldn't promise that you will.

To be <u>capable of</u> doing something is to

- Ⓐ ask someone to do it.
- Ⓑ attempt to do it.
- Ⓒ hope to do it soon.
- Ⓓ be ready and able to do it.

7. Read this sentence from the passage.

You can't <u>alter</u> an event after it has already happened.

In this sentence, <u>alter</u> means

- Ⓐ create.
- Ⓑ change.
- Ⓒ plan.
- Ⓓ attend.

8. Read this sentence from the passage.

It is no use <u>grieving</u> over something that you cannot change.

In this sentence, <u>grieving</u> means

- Ⓐ feeling sad about something.
- Ⓑ trying to change something.
- Ⓒ complaining about something.
- Ⓓ blaming yourself for something.

9. Read these words from the passage.

don't <u>depend</u> on just one person

To <u>depend</u> on a person is to

- Ⓐ love him or her.
- Ⓑ work for him or her.
- Ⓒ count on him or her.
- Ⓓ help him or her.

10. Read these words from the passage.

they felt <u>humiliated</u>

In this sentence, <u>humiliated</u> means very

- Ⓐ embarrassed.
- Ⓑ sad.
- Ⓒ angry.
- Ⓓ messy.

11. Read this sentence from the passage.

Imagine trying to tread on eggs without breaking their <u>fragile</u> shells.

Something that is <u>fragile</u> is very

- Ⓐ tasty.
- Ⓑ pale.
- Ⓒ breakable.
- Ⓓ smooth.

12. Read this sentence from the passage.

The slightest little thing could upset her or make her <u>furious</u>!

What does <u>furious</u> mean in this sentence?

- Ⓐ very late
- Ⓑ somewhat dangerous
- Ⓒ very sad
- Ⓓ very angry

Name: _____   Date: _____

Book 4, Final Test 2 (Lessons 1–20)

Read the passage. Choose the BEST answer for each sentence or question about an underlined word. Then fill in the circle next to your answer.

OLD SAYINGS AND EXPRESSIONS, PART 2

Many old sayings and expressions mention bread, butter, or meat. To *butter someone up* is to flatter that person in order to get your way. *This is my bread and butter* means "This is my <u>livelihood</u>." *Getting to the meat of* a problem or issue means figuring out what its <u>essential</u> parts are. Maybe this expression started because in many soups, stews, and sauces, meat is the most important ingredient.

Since most people like sweets, it is not surprising that there are many expressions about those as well. To *eat humble pie* is to become <u>humble</u> and apologize. *You can't have your cake and eat it, too* means that you must choose one option or the other—you can't have both. Someone who is *as sweet as pie* is, of course, very <u>amiable</u>. A *syrupy story* is a one that is extremely <u>sentimental</u>.

Other kitchen-related sayings and expressions include *Oil and water don't mix*. In other words, people who have very different ideas usually don't <u>blend</u>, or get along. If someone says, "When people hear the news, *the fat will be in the fire*" he or she means that the news will <u>outrage</u> people. When someone escapes one <u>tragic</u> situation only to face a second situation that's even worse, people might say, "*Out of the frying pan and into the fire!*"

Like food, weather is also on most people's minds. English is full of weather-related sayings. When arguing with a <u>pessimist</u>, you might say, "*Every cloud has a silver lining.*" In other words, even a tragedy brings some positive results. If someone is <u>boasting</u>, we can *take the wind out of his sails*, or show that his bragging has no <u>merit</u>.

Though they don't always mean exactly what they say, it can be helpful to know the meanings of sayings and expressions like these. It can also be interesting to find new ways to <u>utilize</u> old sayings or to make up some new sayings and expressions of your own!

1. In this passage, <u>livelihood</u> means

    Ⓐ   flattery.

    Ⓑ   how someone makes a living.

    Ⓒ   important parts.

    Ⓓ   favorite recipes.

2. A problem's <u>essential</u> parts are

    Ⓐ   solutions to that problem.

    Ⓑ   its most important parts.

    Ⓒ   all of its parts.

    Ⓓ   the parts that no one can solve.

3. In this passage, <u>humble</u> means

    Ⓐ   gentle.

    Ⓑ   bitter.

    Ⓒ   sweet.

    Ⓓ   modest.

4. An <u>amiable</u> person is very

    Ⓐ   likable.

    Ⓑ   sentimental.

    Ⓒ   syrupy.

    Ⓓ   talkative.

5. A <u>sentimental</u> love story is

    Ⓐ   too sweet.

    Ⓑ   very funny.

    Ⓒ   complicated.

    Ⓓ   unusual.

6. Which word means about the same as <u>blend</u>?

    Ⓐ   oil

    Ⓑ   water

    Ⓒ   different

    Ⓓ   mix

7. To <u>outrage</u> people is to

    Ⓐ   jeer at them.

    Ⓑ   ignore them.

    Ⓒ   make them angry.

    Ⓓ   entertain them.

8. Something with <u>merit</u> has

    Ⓐ   worth.

    Ⓑ   holes.

    Ⓒ   many parts.

    Ⓓ   an engine.

9. A <u>tragic</u> situation causes

    Ⓐ   fires.

    Ⓑ   suffering.

    Ⓒ   earthquakes.

    Ⓓ   arguments.

10. A <u>pessimist</u> usually

    Ⓐ   dislikes people who brag.

    Ⓑ   expects the worst.

    Ⓒ   talks on and on in a boring manner.

    Ⓓ   jeers at others.

11. To <u>boast</u> is to

    Ⓐ   sail.

    Ⓑ   expect the worst.

    Ⓒ   brag.

    Ⓓ   praise others.

12. Which of the following means about the same as <u>utilize</u>?

    Ⓐ   excite

    Ⓑ   begin

    Ⓒ   use

    Ⓓ   destroy

Name: _____   Date: _____

Book 4, Final Test 3 (Lessons 1–20)

Read the passage below. Choose the best answer for each item that follows. Then fill in the circle next to your answer.

ROMEO AND JULIET, PART 1

William Shakespeare lived in England in the 1500s and 1600s. He wrote 37 plays that people still read, perform, and study. One of his most famous <u>tragedies</u> is called *Romeo and Juliet*, a story about two teenagers who fall in love. Sadly, they are "star-crossed," or doomed from the start. Here is the beginning of the tale. To find out how it <u>concludes</u>, you will have to read the play or see it performed.

Romeo and Juliet takes place in Verona, Italy. Two families, the Montagues and the Capulets, have a bitter, ongoing quarrel between them. No one even seems to know what started the <u>dispute</u> in the first place. Their <u>feud</u> causes many problems in Verona, because the families and their friends are fighting violently. Prince Escalus, Verona's ruler, says that if any more people are seen fighting, they will be <u>arrested</u> and killed.

Young Romeo, a Montague, is feeling <u>forlorn</u>. He is in love with a woman named Rosaline who won't marry him. As he tells his friend Benvolio how sad he is, the two happen to meet a Capulet servant in the street. The man is carrying the guest list for a costume party at the Capulet house that evening. The servant is ordered to invite everyone on the list, though, unfortunately, he cannot read. He <u>implores</u> Romeo to help him. Romeo reads the list aloud and discovers that Rosaline is invited, so Benvolio <u>persuades</u> Romeo to go to the party in disguise. "You should <u>attend</u> the party," says Benvolio. "You'll be able to <u>contrast</u> Rosaline with the other guests at the party. Then you'll see that she isn't so wonderful, after all." Romeo disagrees—he thinks Rosaline is exquisite—but he decides to go anyway.

Romeo arrives at the party with a mask covering his face. Standing on the <u>fringe</u> of the guests, he spies a beautiful girl. She is Juliet, the daughter of old Capulet, the host of the party. Romeo finds Juliet's grace and beauty so <u>astounding</u> that he falls in love with her at first sight. He instantly forgets about Rosaline.

1. Read these words from the passage.

   one of his most famous <u>tragedies</u> is called *Romeo and Juliet*

   In this passage, <u>tragedies</u> means

   - Ⓐ earthquakes.
   - Ⓑ hurricanes.
   - Ⓒ humorous plays.
   - Ⓓ plays that end sadly.

2. Read this sentence from the passage.

   To find out how it <u>concludes</u>, you will have to read the play or see it performed.

   In this passage, <u>concludes</u> means

   - Ⓐ develops.
   - Ⓑ ends.
   - Ⓒ works.
   - Ⓓ begins.

3. Read this sentence from the passage.

   No one even seems to know what started the <u>dispute</u> in the first place.

   A <u>dispute</u> is

   - Ⓐ an argument.
   - Ⓑ a family.
   - Ⓒ a friendship.
   - Ⓓ an idea.

4. Read this sentence from the passage.

   Their <u>feud</u> causes many problems in Verona.

   The <u>feud</u> between the Montagues and Capulets is

   - Ⓐ a fence.
   - Ⓑ a contrast.
   - Ⓒ a long, bitter quarrel.
   - Ⓓ a friendly competition.

5. Read these words from the passage.

if any more people are caught fighting, they will be <u>arrested</u>

In this sentence, <u>arrested</u> means

    (A) forced to leave a place.

    (B) told to stop.

    (C) separated from each other.

    (D) seized and charged with a crime.

6. Read this sentence from the passage.

Young Romeo, a Montague, is feeling <u>forlorn</u>.

This sentence means that Romeo feels

    (A) worried about being in love.

    (B) angry with someone.

    (C) sad and lonely.

    (D) excited about meeting someone.

7. Read this sentence from the passage.

He <u>implores</u> Romeo to help him.

In this sentence, <u>implores</u> means

    (A) begs.

    (B) hires.

    (C) commands.

    (D) directs.

8. Read these words from the passage.

Benvolio <u>persuades</u> Romeo to go to the party

What does Benvolio do?

    (A) He implores Romeo to go.

    (B) He commands Romeo to go.

    (C) He convinces Romeo to go.

    (D) He suggests that Romeo stay away from the party.

9. Read this sentence from the passage.

"You should <u>attend</u> the party," says Benvolio.

To <u>attend</u> a party is to

- Ⓐ feel excited about it.
- Ⓑ invite guests to it.
- Ⓒ sneak in without an invitation.
- Ⓓ go to it.

10. Read this sentence from the passage.

"You'll be able to <u>contrast</u> Rosaline with the other guests at the party."

Benvolio means that Romeo will be able to

- Ⓐ find guests who are exactly like Rosaline.
- Ⓑ find guests who are friends with Rosaline.
- Ⓒ find differences between Rosaline and the other guests.
- Ⓓ find similarities between Rosaline and the other guests.

11. Read this sentence from the passage.

Standing on the <u>fringe</u> of the guests, he spies a beautiful girl.

This sentence means that Romeo is standing

- Ⓐ in the middle of the group.
- Ⓑ at the edge of the group.
- Ⓒ right next to Juliet.
- Ⓓ far away from everyone else.

12. Read this sentence from the passage.

Romeo finds Juliet's grace and beauty so <u>astounding</u> that he falls in love with her at first sight.

Which word could you substitute for <u>astounding</u> in this sentence?

- Ⓐ humorous
- Ⓑ amazing
- Ⓒ appalling
- Ⓓ dainty

Book 4, Final Test 4 (Lessons 1–20)

Read the passage below. Choose the best answer for each item that follows. Then fill in the circle next to your answer.

ROMEO AND JULIET, PART 2

Unfortunately, Juliet's cousin Tybalt is also at the Capulet party. Tybalt <u>detests</u> all Montagues and he <u>recognizes</u> Romeo right away. Tybalt is <u>outraged</u> that a Montague would attend a Capulet party. Meanwhile, Romeo manages to <u>approach</u> Juliet. He tells the girl how <u>devoted</u> he is to her. To his delight, Romeo discovers that Juliet loves him, too. Soon Romeo finds out that Juliet is a Capulet, and she finds out that he is a Montague. This news <u>appalls</u> both of them. Each feels that it is a great <u>misfortune</u> to be in love with an enemy.

Later, Romeo climbs the wall around Juliet's garden. Juliet comes out onto her balcony and, thinking that she is alone, <u>utters</u> her private thoughts out loud. She wishes Romeo would forget about the feud between their families and marry her. At this, Romeo appears and <u>proposes</u>. The two <u>embrace</u> again and again. They make plans to communicate through Juliet's nurse, her caretaker and friend. The nurse will meet Romeo the next morning, and Romeo will set a time and place for the marriage.

Romeo and Juliet's secret marriage plans work out fine. Romeo's old teacher, Friar Laurence, marries them. The newlyweds are filled with <u>bliss</u>. Unfortunately, the tragic <u>portion</u> of the story is just beginning.

1. Tybalt <u>detests</u> all Montagues. This means that he

    Ⓐ   is their cousin.

    Ⓑ   doesn't know any of them.

    Ⓒ   hates them.

    Ⓓ   is afraid of them.

2. Tybalt <u>recognizes</u> Romeo. This means that he

    Ⓐ   slays Romeo.

    Ⓑ   remembers who Romeo is.

    Ⓒ   welcomes Romeo to the party.

    Ⓓ   argues with Romeo.

3. Tybalt was <u>outraged</u> that Romeo was at the party. This means that Tybalt was

    Ⓐ   honored.

    Ⓑ   very excited.

    Ⓒ   surprised.

    Ⓓ   very angry.

4. Romeo is <u>devoted</u> to Juliet. This means that he

    Ⓐ   knows she is a Capulet.

    Ⓑ   loves her very much.

    Ⓒ   asks her to marry him.

    Ⓓ   wants to work as her servant.

5. Romeo manages to <u>approach</u> Juliet. What does <u>approach</u> mean in this sentence?

    Ⓐ   get closer to.

    Ⓑ   promise to love.

    Ⓒ   detest.

    Ⓓ   propose.

6. Juliet is <u>appalled</u> to learn that Romeo is a Montague. Which word means about the same as <u>appalled</u>?

    Ⓐ   shocked

    Ⓑ   humiliated

    Ⓒ   blissful

    Ⓓ   content

7. Which means about the same as <u>misfortune</u>?

    Ⓐ   merit

    Ⓑ   inconvenience

    Ⓒ   bad luck

    Ⓓ   joke

8. Juliet <u>utters</u> her private thoughts. This means that she

    Ⓐ   dreams them.

    Ⓑ   speaks them.

    Ⓒ   thinks them.

    Ⓓ   worries about them.

9. Romeo and Juliet <u>embrace</u> again and again. This means that they

    Ⓐ   promise to love each other.

    Ⓑ   hug each other.

    Ⓒ   call each other sweet names.

    Ⓓ   announce their happiness.

10. <u>Bliss</u> is great

    Ⓐ   sorrow.

    Ⓑ   outrage.

    Ⓒ   curiosity.

    Ⓓ   happiness.

11. They have no <u>misgivings</u>. This means that they

    Ⓐ   want to forget about the feud between the families.

    Ⓑ   want to forgive their parents.

    Ⓒ   have given a present to the wrong person.

    Ⓓ   have no doubts about their marriage.

12. A <u>portion</u> of a story is

    Ⓐ   the beginning.

    Ⓑ   one part of it.

    Ⓒ   one of the characters.

    Ⓓ   the ending.

Answer Key

Lesson 1 Test

1. B
2. A
3. C
4. C
5. C
6. D
7. B
8. A
9. D
10. C
11. A
12. D
13. A
14. C
15. B
16. C
17. C
18. C
19. D
20. C
21. B
22. A
23. C
24. B
25. D
26. A
27. B
28. B
29. B
30. C
31. A
32. C
33. B
34. B
35. C

Lesson 2 Test

1. C
2. A
3. B
4. D
5. D
6. A
7. B
8. D
9. C
10. A
11. D
12. A
13. A
14. C
15. A
16. B

17. B
18. C
19. C
20. D
21. B
22. C
23. B
24. A
25. B
26. C
27. C
28. A
29. A
30. C

Lesson 3 Test

1. C
2. B
3. C
4. A
5. A
6. C
7. B
8. A
9. C
10. A
11. C
12. C
13. C
14. A
15. C
16. C
17. A
18. B
19. D
20. C
21. B
22. B
23. D
24. A
25. C
26. C
27. B
28. B
29. A
30. B
31. B
32. D

Lesson 4 Test

1. B
2. C
3. D
4. B
5. A

6. B
7. D
8. B
9. A
10. D
11. B
12. A
13. D
14. A
15. C
16. D
17. C
18. D
19. A
20. C
21. D
22. A
23. C
24. B
25. D
26. C
27. B
28. D
29. B
30. A
31. B
32. C
33. C
34. D
35. B
36. A
37. C
38. A

Lesson 5 Test

1. B
2. D
3. B
4. A
5. B
6. A
7. D
8. B
9. A
10. B
11. C
12. C
13. D
14. B
15. C
16. D
17. D
18. C
19. A
20. D

21. B
22. B
23. C
24. B
25. A
26. C
27. B
28. B
29. A

Lesson 6 Test

1. A
2. C
3. A
4. A
5. C
6. A
7. B
8. A
9. D
10. D
11. A
12. B
13. A
14. C
15. B
16. C
17. B
18. B
19. C
20. A
21. B
22. B
23. A
24. C
25. B
26. C

Lesson 7 Test

1. C
2. B
3. C
4. C
5. C
6. D
7. A
8. B
9. D
10. A
11. B
12. C
13. D
14. C
15. D
16. B

Answer Key

17. C
18. D
19. C
20. B
21. D
22. C
23. D
24. D
25. B
26. A
27. D
28. C
29. D
30. A
31 B
32 C

Lesson 8 Test

1. C
2. D
3. C
4. D
5. C
6. C
7. C
8. D
9. A
10. D
11. B
12. B
13. B
14. C
15. A
16. D
17. B
18. B
19. D
20. B
21. D
22. C
23. B
24. D
25. C
26. D
27. C
28. A
29. B
30. B

Lesson 9 Test

1. B
2. D
3. C
4. A
5. B

6. B
7. D
8. C
9. A
10. A
11. B
12. D
13. A
14. C
15. B
16. C
17. B
18. D
19. A
20. C
21. A
22. C
23. B
24. C
25. D
26. D
27. A

Lesson 10 Test

1. B
2. D
3. B
4. A
5. B
6. A
7. B
8. C
9. C
10. D
11. B
12. B
13. B
14. C
15. D
16. B
17. B
18. C
19. A
20. A
21. C
22. D
23. D
24. A
25. C
26. A
27. D
28. D

Midterm Test 1
(Lessons 1–10)

1. B
2. C
3. A
4. D
5. B
6. B
7. C
8. A
9. B
10. C
11. D
12. B

Midterm Test 2
(Lessons 1–10)

1. A
2. C
3. C
4. C
5. B
6. D
7. D
8. A
9. B
10. D
11. C
12. B

Lesson 11 Test

1. D
2. B
3. D
4. C
5. D
6. C
7. B
8. D
9. A
10. B
11. C
12. B
13. B
14. D
15. D
16. C
17. C
18. A
19. C
20. D
21. B
22. C
23. B

24. A
25. B
26. C
27. A
28. D
29. D
30. B
31. D
32. D
33. A

Lesson 12 Test

1. B
2. B
3. C
4. B
5. D
6. A
7. C
8. A
9. C
10. B
11. D
12. C
13. A
14. D
15. B
16. D
17. C
18. C
19. D
20. D
21. A
22. B
23. A
24. C
25. D
26. A
27. C
28. D
29. C
30. D
31. A

Lesson 13 Test

1. B
2. A
3. B
4. D
5. C
6. B
7. B
8. A
9. D

Answer Key

10. C
11. A
12. D
13. B
14. A
15. A
16. B
17. C
18. B
19. B
20. C
21. B
22. C
23. C
24. B
25. D
26. B
27. A
28. B
29. D
30. C
31. D
32. D
33. C
34. D

Lesson 14 Test

1. D
2. B
3. A
4. D
5. A
6. B
7. A
8. B
9. C
10. A
11. C
12. B
13. C
14. D
15. B
16. A
17. C
18. B
19. C
20. D
21. B
22. A
23. C
24. C
25. D
26. B
27. A
28. D

Lesson 15 Test

1. C
2. B
3. A
4. C
5. A
6. A
7. B
8. A
9. D
10. A
11. B
12. B
13. B
14. C
15. A
16. A
17. C
18. D
19. C
20. A
21. C
22. B
23. A
24. A
25. D
26. B
27. B
28. A
29. C
30. D

Lesson 16 Test

1. D
2. A
3. C
4. C
5. B
6. A
7. A
8. D
9. C
10. B
11. A
12. C
13. C
14. B
15. C
16. A
17. C
18. D
19. A
20. B
21. A
22. B

23. D
24. B
25. D
26. C
27. B
28. A

Lesson 17 Test

1. A
2. B
3. D
4. D
5. C
6. C
7. C
8. B
9. A
10. B
11. C
12. A
13. A
14. B
15. B
16. A
17. C
18. C
19. B
20. A
21. B
22. C
23. A
24. B
25. A
26. A
27. C
28. B
29. D
30. B
31. D
32. C

Lesson 18 Test

1. B
2. C
3. A
4. A
5. D
6. A
7. B
8. C
9. B
10. C
11. D
12. A
13. C

14. B
15. C
16. C
17. D
18. A
19. B
20. D
21. C
22. B
23. C
24. A
25. B
26. D

Lesson 19 Test

1. D
2. B
3. B
4. C
5. B
6. A
7. B
8. D
9. C
10. B
11. B
12. D
13. C
14. A
15. B
16. A
17. B
18. C
19. B
20. C
21. A
22. B
23. B
24. D
25. B
26. D
27. C
28. B

Lesson 20 Test

1. B
2. B
3. D
4. C
5. A
6. C
7. C
8. B
9. A
10. C

Answer Key

11. C
12. D
13. D
14. B
15. A
16. B
17. C
18. B
19. B
20. D
21. B
22. C
23. B
24. C
25. A
26. B
27. A
28. C
29. B
30. D
31. D
32. C
33. A

Final Test 1
(Lessons 1–20)

1. C
2. C
3. A
4. A
5. C
6. D
7. B
8. A
9. C
10. A
11. C
12. D

Final Test 2
(Lessons 1–20)

1. B
2. B
3. D
4. A
5. A
6. D
7. C
8. A
9. B
10. B
11. C
12. C

Final Test 3
(Lessons 1–20)

1. D
2. B
3. A
4. C
5. D
6. C
7. A
8. C
9. D
10. C
11. B
12. B

Final Test 4
(Lessons 1–20)

1. C
2. B
3. D
4. B
5. A
6. A
7. C
8. B
9. B
10. D
11. D
12. B